THE DBT SKILLS WORKBOOK FOR
TEENS

ANGER
MANAGEMENT

Develop Essential Coping Skills To
Manage Angry Outbursts And Gain
Self Control Through Effective Self-
Regulation Techniques

M.A. MARTINE

LEGAL NOTICE

DISCLAIMER NOTICE

GET THIS EXCLUSIVE

5-minute Audio Guided Meditation

*To help safely **MANAGE YOUR TEEN'S** sudden emotional meltdown.*

and more mindfulness resources...

JOURNALS & SELF-CARE PLANERS

COLORING BOOKS

SCAN QR CODE TO GET YOUR COPY

TABLE OF CONTENTS

TABLE OF CONTENTS

TABLE OF CONTENTS

TABLE OF CONTENTS

INTRODUCTION

I t started like any other day, but it ended excitingly uncomfortable after taking a vastly more disruptive turn. I found myself on the precipice of transformation. It was the day when it all came tumbling down like a ton of bricks. All the slammed doors and the splinters of broken glasses or mugs—whatever were the closest that moment when my anger became so intolerable, I knew throwing something was the only way to decompress—that left a trail of destruction from my teenage years, right up to my early 20s.

While it was evident that my anger was getting out of control long before I turned 16, the most memories I have of my behavior being erratic and fueled with rage is from the year I was that age. I think what made it even worse that year was the idea of it being my "sweet 16," and I couldn't identify anything sweet to the age or me being that age.

I hated school, I hated my family, and I had no friends and hated that too. But, then again, I wasn't that fond of people either, so heaven knows why I hated not having friends. Even then, that wasn't the worst part of my life. I could remove myself from all those things—escape them as I often did, sitting, simmering in my own misery behind closed doors in my room. What I couldn't run from, which made me probably hate it even more, was myself. I remember looking in the mirror, and I couldn't see anything about myself that I liked no matter how I searched. Mom would say, "You have such beautiful hair," or, "Your skin is so healthy," but it meant absolutely nothing to me. I couldn't see it, and it felt like she pitied me. I just knew that I hated my appearance, thought my skills were useless, and couldn't even stand hearing my voice.

Let's just say that much hating happened during my teenage years. For the longest time, I thought I was a harsh & intolerable person with no emotion to express other than anger.

It was only much later that I learned that anger is often nothing other than a blanket used to cover an immense pain rooted so deep inside that it seems impossible to reach. A pain without cause or reason &, therefore, so much harder to ease. I remember thinking—no, knowing—that someone would hurt me, disappoint me, or—the worst—reject me. But I refused to allow that to happen to me, so I turned to anger. See, if you reject them first, they cannot reject you.

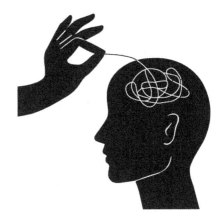

STANDING ON THE PRECIPICE OF TRANSFORMATION

I remember that day well when I couldn't do it anymore. See, when you allow a raging fire of anger to burn inside you for too long, it ravishes all that keeps you upright and offers stability, and then one day, you collapse. I am unsure whether, on the day I collapsed, the debris of my being also extinguished the raging fire within or if perhaps there was nothing more left to burn. So, I started to seek a way out of the ash and smoke of my smoldering existence.

It all happened by chance. I had to escape, and I walked out of my apartment, out of another relationship, another dream to die on its own as I wandered the streets of my neighborhood. It was cold, so I grabbed a coffee from the local vendor. We were familiar with each other as regular clients sometimes turn into friends, and he introduced me to his friend chatting at his stand. She was pretty, but I found her kindness uncomfortable and didn't know what to say. It didn't matter, she started talking, and strangely enough, she didn't stop until she got me hooked on a thing called dialectical behavior therapy (DBT). When I walked away from her—finally—I couldn't forget our conversation. I wanted to know more. She was a starry-eyed student in her field, and her passion for her subject was so contagious that even miserable me caught on. For the first time in my life, it felt like maybe things could be different.

Now, almost a decade later, I know that day was my crossroad day. It was the day when a stranger saved me from myself. I've never seen her again, not even bumped into her by accident. But what she did for me was introduce me to a therapy that changed my life. Her passion for helping others attracted my interest to the point where I was keen to learn more. I studied everything I could find about emotional intelligence, anger management, and how mindfulness can transform your life. I've read more than 100 books on the topic in 1 year and devoured every video I could find to watch.

Each time I completed working through another bit of information, I would diligently apply the skills and techniques I'd learned. I wouldn't stop until I could fix every cognitive distortion overshadowing my life—yep, eventually, I became familiar with terms to describe the challenges I was facing more elegantly. DBT became more than my lifeline with which I could pull myself out of the misery I referred to as my "life." It also turned into my life purpose, my passion.

MEET ME AT THE CROSSROAD

Today, I am helping many other teens discover their anger's underlying causes. These teenagers have so much in common with the teenage version of me, a person who was in so much pain, even though there was no apparent reason for me to be hurt or angry. It was also a version of me who was destructive & hurtful with my words and actions.

My journey required intensive reading and self-study. I am grateful that I was introduced to this type of therapy by a random stranger in a random act, putting a stop to my familiar routine of discarding all that was precious before it was time to let go of it. I will never be able to make it up to the coffee-stand girl who scooped me up emotionally when I was at my lowest, but I can—and I did—commit myself to formulating all the snippets of information into a unity that is easy to understand. It is this unity of knowledge, a collection of practical skills and steps, that I am presenting to you. As you progress through the pages, you'll notice subtle changes. You'll become aware of how the anger dissipates to make room for other emotions. Once you acknowledge these emotions, you can finally process them and let go of the burden they lay upon you.

However, if you know someone, a teenager engulfed in unidentified emotions that they reflect as anger, this book will also bring you the necessary tools you seek to help them. Over the past 12 years, I've been diligently working towards finding the most practical approach to present the knowledge I know will make a difference to your life, as it did to mine and the lives of the many patients I've seen as a clinical psychologist. I started to have conversations with therapists working with teenagers, and the ideas we shared inspired me to present the information so that this book can also be a helpful tool to the therapist who's agonizing over the lack of progress they are making in their sessions too.

There is one thing I regret, though: losing so much time wandering without purpose and being angry without a cause. Most of my teenage years are trapped in one dark and dreary blur.

Time is precious and limited, and we never know when the last day for you or a dear loved one will come. I know now that I would hate it if time had run out on me before I could gain control over my emotions and, subsequently, my life.

I don't know where you are on your journey in life, whether you are ready to let go of your anger and improve how you manage your emotions. I don't know if you seek a solution and the process found this book. Nor do I know if this book randomly landed in your field of interest, like I unknowingly stumbled into the answers I've been seeking entirely randomly. You need to determine whether you are ready to make that change, let go of your anger, and free yourself from the hurt. It doesn't require any significant changes in your life. But, through consistent minor changes, you will gradually start to experience a shift of epic proportions as you steadily begin to levitate toward a life of contentment, joy, satisfaction, hope, & anticipation over the future.

Are you at your crossroad? Is now a good time to unfold the possibilities of your future? Let's take the first step to exiting the familiar emotional turmoil.

CHAPTER 1: ANGER AND YOU

> 66 Where there is anger, there is always pain underneath. 99
>
> – Eckhart Tolle

Do you sometimes feel guilty for being angry so often? The emotion of anger is often vilified by the wider population. It almost comes across as perfectly normal to feel any other emotion—and you may even be encouraged to be more in tune with these emotions—as long as it is not anger, for being angry is "bad." That is not the case at all. Anger is just another emotion like sadness, joy, excitement, or jealousy—the latter which doesn't even have as bad a reputation as anger. This tendency is often explained that anger has a bad reputation due to how angry people behave while in this state. Of course, this is a questionable statement too, for have you ever seen how erratic someone overcome with jealousy can be?

But let's stop tripling around the emotion's reputation & jump right in to explore what anger is.

DEFINING ANGER

After consulting a few expert definitions of anger, it is safe to attach the following attributes to the emotion.

Anger is an intense human emotion, often causing a great sense of animosity towards someone or something. It is often accompanied by irritation, frustration, annoyance, hostility, and an increased level of stress. It is an emotion everyone feels at some time in their lives—some more often than others.

Anger is often triggered by emotional pain but can also result from being disturbed, interrupted, or threatened. Anger can present itself in various degrees of severity.

Up to this point, these attributes are still aligned with the characteristics of most other negative emotions.

The difference comes in the last characteristic of anger that I need to highlight: If anger is not managed well, it can lead to erratic behavior, stepping over the boundaries of what is socially acceptable to the point where you are making yourself guilty of criminality.

DANNY'S STORY

Danny's entire team has already left the changing rooms and is probably almost home, but he is still sitting on the bench stuck in his gear.

Football is his life. It was the one thing his dad taught him before he got sick. It is the only reason he comes to school and works hard on his subjects to get good grades, just to stay on the team.

His phone beeping distracts his thoughts. He realizes how late it is and that he needs to get home. Now, he has to tell his mother and younger brother what a failure he is. Danny gets up, and as he does, his anger breaks loose while he remains incapable of taking control. The janitor walked in on the mess; every mirror in the changing room was shattered on the floor. It is also where he finds Danny huddling over his broken hand. The pain that shuddered through every single bone from the impact when his hand made a dent in his locker door brought the destruction to an end.

> **Danny's story can also have another outcome.**

His phone beeping distracts his thoughts. He realizes how late it is and that he needs to get home. Now, he has to tell his mother and younger brother he isn't playing on Saturday. As he takes his gear off, his mind is consumed, searching for solutions to his problem. He'll check in with Coach about why he isn't playing and ask him for extra exercises to improve his game. He'll just have to practice more, work harder, and make Coach see that the team needs him. That will make his dad proud. That is what he'll tell his mother and little bro.

The two versions of Danny's story teach us one more valuable lesson about anger: We have the choice to use our rage destructively or constructively. The outcome you choose will depend on how well you can manage your anger as well as your capability to recognize the underlying causes of why you are responding in this manner.

WHAT IS YOUR ANGER TYPE?

For some, the topic of the number of ways how anger manifests is still a lively debate. While some experts state the correct number is 8, others distinguish 12 types of anger. I prefer to highlight the following 10 types, and I encourage you to explore each type discerningly to determine with which you identify the most vividly.

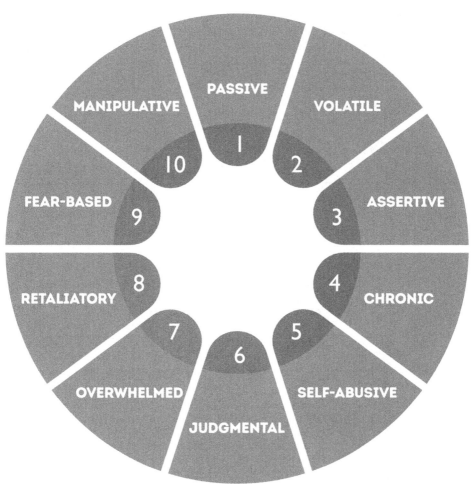

1. PASSIVE

Passive anger can be hard to distinguish as it doesn't manifest similarly to most other forms of aggression. It is not accompanied by a significant outburst of emotions, but it can be extremely hostile. The person who is passively angry reverts to sarcasm, being purposefully forgetful, dragging their feet to get things done, or may revert to a range of other ways to express their anger without being upfront about it. This type of anger is often internalized and can therefore be highly toxic to the angry person. Typical behaviors identified with this type of anger include binge eating, excessive drinking, panic attacks, and even self-harm. It is the opposite of the following kind of anger—volatile anger. In volatile anger, the angry person takes out their rage externally, but for the passive-aggressive person, the rage occurs internally.

2. VOLATILE

Typically, this person would make it clear to all that they are angry, and they do this by portraying explosive behavior. We find this type of anger right on the other end of the spectrum from passive anger, as here, the angry person isn't internalizing any rage at the moment they explode. Still, these explosions can be caused by prolonged suppression of their emotions. Like a volcano, they will be brewing underneath the surface for quite some time and then explode entirely unpredictably. This explosion can be triggered by something insignificant; typically, they cool down rapidly after letting off their steam. Danny's volatile and destructive explosion in the changing rooms has a lot resembling this type of anger outburst.

3. ASSERTIVE

Assertive anger is widely considered to be the most constructive form of anger. The feelings that immerse during this type of anger are usually applied constructively to bring about change to the situation, causing frustration, irritation, or any other negative emotion. We seldom witness confrontations, physical outbursts, or even internalization of this anger, as the angered person applies the energy of their anger constructively. Danny's portrayal of rage in the second version of his story can be classified as assertive anger.

4. CHRONIC

Many parents of teenagers would claim they are dealing with this type of anger in their homes. It is the type of anger that seems persistently present and can manifest as irritation and frustration with others and yourself. Rather than witnessing severe and abrupt outbursts, the person with chronic anger appears to be constantly in a bad mood, giving even those who are merely innocent bystanders in their life a piece of their mind. While no anger ever positively impacts your overall well-being, it is particularly bad as it keeps the angered individual in this state for a prolonged period.

5. SELF-ABUSIVE

We find guilt and shame at the core of this type of anger. Together with low self-esteem, the circle of negativity continues to expand, becoming more profound and affecting more parts of the person's life and, eventually, their health and well-being. At times, the angry person may react and have an outburst, increasing the isolation and guilt already burdening them. Other ways the angry person may express their internal anger are through self-harm, negative self-talk, or eating disorders.

6. JUDGMENTAL

Considering themselves in a morally superior position, those suffering from judgmental anger perceive their anger as righteous. They will blast you with verbal criticism if you are the victim of their rage. They would consider you to be the one at fault for being or behaving unjustly, according to their moral compass.

While this is a harsh and often highly distorted form of anger, it can be applied constructively to bring about change in toxic situations. However, when you portray this kind of anger, your actions and approach towards others would likely serve as a tool to isolate you from others, causing you to lack social interaction and support. This type of anger is also closely linked to Asperger's syndrome and is a pretty common way for those on this spectrum to express their anger (Bajori, 2019).

7. OVERWHELMED

Depending on your outlook on life, it can be easy to agree that life is challenging at the best of times. If you are the kind of person who would rather see the cup half empty than half full, you would be more prone to experience this kind of anger. It is likely to reach a peak when you persistently feel overwhelmed and overstressed and when life is generally pressing down on you. Do you often think that life is just too demanding and that you don't have the energy to continue?

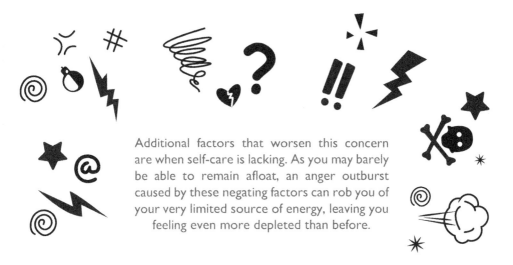

Additional factors that worsen this concern are when self-care is lacking. As you may barely be able to remain afloat, an anger outburst caused by these negating factors can rob you of your very limited source of energy, leaving you feeling even more depleted than before.

8. MANIPULATIVE

Anger can be used to get others to do what you want. You can come across as threatening when your angry outburst is highly volatile. Due to the fear you instill in those around you, they may be intimidated by you and comply with your demands only because they want to defuse the situation. Evidently, this is not a healthy situation to be in, as your relationships are somewhat toxic. The person using anger in their favor in this manner is always aware of the impact of their outbursts on others. However, they may not realize that people, even your loved ones, can only take so much before walking away from you, leaving you rejected by others due to how you utilize your anger to their detriment.

9. FEAR-BASED

While this specific type of anger is connected to fear alone, the mechanics of this kind of anger is very much the same for many other emotions that may leave you vulnerable. The choice you are making is, rather, to express your feelings in the form of fear, as it hurts less than acknowledging that you are scared, hurt, lonely, or any other negative emotion that you are concerned may cause you to come across as weak. Examples of this kind of anger are when you see how a younger sibling runs across the road and is almost hit by a car; instead of expressing gratitude for making it across fine, you shout at them for being stupid. Or, when you are feeling hurt by a friend for blowing you off on the plans you were looking forward to, you become mean towards the friend and may even be a little passive-aggressive not to admit that you are feeling hurt by what they did.

10.RETALIATORY

This kind of anger is based on the principle of an eye for an eye. You've made me angry by hurting me or taking something I treasure away from me, and now I'll get you back and take something from you. At the core of this kind of anger, we find the need to revenge for something that we perceive as dreadful that has happened. It can often present itself in purposeful actions as you try to get back at someone else. It is seldom that this kind of anger presents itself as an outburst. No, it is much more aligned with a subtle approach that may stretch over days, weeks, or even months as you plot your plan to get back at someone else.

Which of these 10 types of anger can you identify with in your life? You may experience a combination of different types of anger. But then again, it is also possible that you find yourself in a position where admitting to being guilty of any of these types is simply too hard to do right now. Openly admitting that you have an anger problem can be challenging. After all, it is one thing to be painfully aware that your anger is out of control when you are alone, but admitting it to others is entirely different. If you aren't ready yet to share this with anyone else, then do so in the privacy of your mind, just as long as you take the first and vital step of admitting the challenge you are facing as it is where your healing journey starts.

THE MOST COMMON TRIGGERS OF ANGER

Anger triggers are no different than any other type of emotional trigger. These triggers can be insignificant, sparking an emotional response in the person.

Triggers can also take on various forms: from scents or aromas; to music or sounds; images; experiences; or anything else that awakens a memory of a bad experience or reminds you of someone, causing a deep and intense emotional experience. In the case of anger triggers, the particular emotion is always anger.

By understanding that these triggers exist and have a negative effect on you and by identifying your unique triggers, you can start to address them more constructively. While some may prefer to avoid exposure to these triggers at all costs—and it may be helpful to a certain degree—it is not necessarily the most wholesome approach to the matter. Effectively, you are not resolving anything and are merely limiting your life, as it may happen that you rather avoid certain situations and rob yourself of experiences.

A much more effective approach is to determine the roots of these triggers and the underlying causes of concern, so that you can address these matters and disempower the trigger from the hold it has on your life.

Some of the most common examples of anger triggers are witnessing or experiencing any of the following:

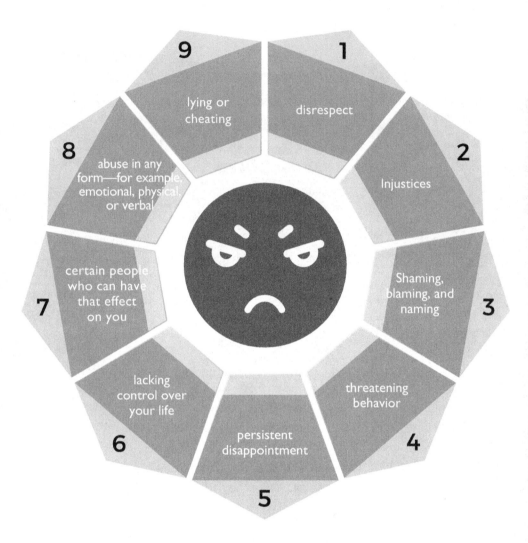

These triggers can originate in events that took place during our childhood years; past events; life experiences; our values & belief systems; or even from believing stories we are told.

An effective way to identify your triggers is by keeping a journal where you can record the anger outburst that you have had and by capturing the details of the events preceding your outburst. Once you've collected the details surrounding these events over a period, you'll be able to notice certain patterns; these will guide you to determine the common factors that were present before the event, usually identifying your triggers.

UNDERSTANDING THE ANGER CYCLE

When we are angry or even witness someone who is, it feels like anger is just one pool of steaming hot and melted emotions. It can be easy to be so overwhelmed at that moment that we struggle to see that anger is not one single event but a series of events or stages. The anger cycle is an umbrella term referring to this series of events or stages.

Once we can dissect the cycle into greater detail and learn how to identify in which stage we or those near to us are, we can change our approach and have a positive impact on the outcome. As we delve a little deeper into the mechanics of this cycle and how it all fits together, I want you to observe how every stage follows the previous in a very natural order, but also to be aware of the fact that during any of these stages, you can step in, change the course you are on, or impact the angered person in such a manner that the outcome can be completely different.

STAGE 1–TRIGGERED

The number of variables that serve as triggers is limitless. A trigger can be an event, a specific treatment, a reminder, or anything from various factors that trigger your anger. It is the initial phase where it all starts. As this is the primary stage of the anger cycle, it is also the most desired stage to put an end to it.

However, there is a saying that nobody notices when you are being provoked, only when you respond or react. It is most likely the most frustrating part of the entire anger cycle.

You are feeling provoked, often by the repeated comments or actions of another, and while you are being offended or treated unfairly, nobody comes to save you. They don't even notice what is happening to you and what you must endure. However, the moment you react, you have the entire room's attention.

One of the most common places where I've seen the frustration of not being noticed boil over into a hot mess, only to be seen once the person being provoked reacts, is in schools.

A bully can torment a child for a long time, and the bully's victim may take one knock on the chin after another, holding their composure. As they are only human, one day, they snap. That is the day when all chaos breaks loose, and instantly, the victim is made out to be the perpetrator while the bullied is considered the wronged one onto whom everyone rains their empathy.

STAGE 2-BUILDUP

This stage is trapped between the moment of being triggered and the response. It is a time when the anger escalates. Your thoughts become more negative. It is an emotional response that manifests physically too, as your eyes widen, eyebrows twist, muscles tense, and your tone of voice may go up a pitch or two. You can feel your heart beating faster, maybe there is a slight shiver in your hands, and your breathing becomes rapid. Remember that anger, like any other emotion, presents itself on all levels of your being.

This stage can last only for a few seconds or, in the case of the school bully tormenting you day after day for several weeks, it can have a much more gradual buildup. In the latter case, you may feel how anger rises in your physical being every time you walk into your school but manage to control these emotions. However, due to failing efforts to resolve the cause of your anger, the buildup only increases as time passes.

STAGE 3-EXPLOSION

When you arrive at this stage of the anger cycle, there is little chance of turning back—your mind and body are prepared to fight. As a matter of fact, fighting may seem the only solution to shake the tension that has your entire being in a grip.

The desire to seek relief that will restore your internal calm is so strong that all reason and rationality dissipate from the situation. You strike out, and the pressure is gone.

STAGE 4-RECOVERY

It's over. You've said what you had to say. You did what was necessary to relieve the buildup inside. Physically, your entire state returns to normal.

Adrenaline levels, heart rate, and blood pressure all return to normal, and as the biological equilibrium is restored, rationality and reason return, taking you to the next and final stage of the anger cycle: regret.

STAGE 5-REGRET

This is the stage where you come back to your senses. As you analyze the situation and determine what has just happened, why you were so out of control and blindly infuriated, it dawns on you with absolute clarity that there were different ways you could've resolved the matter. Regret is always too late. Now, you realize that you should've addressed the concern when you initially identified the trigger or realized that you were being provoked. You should've reported your bully to the school administration, discussed the matter with a school counselor, or addressed your concerns with your parents. While you believed you were strong enough to overcome the challenges of being triggered, you now know you were wrong.

One of the two most predominant mistakes we make regarding anger is to confuse it with aggression. In contrast with aggression, anger is a healthy emotion to experience if we manage it effectively. The second is that we underestimate how intense anger can be and to what extent it will override our rationale, principles, values, and beliefs if we don't manage it effectively.

Stage 1 remains the most desired and possibly effective time to take action and change your direction. This is true not only for your anger but also for stepping in and changing the outcome of someone else's anger.

DIGGING DEEPER

The secret to any successful relationship is having a fair balance between giving and taking. The success of this book is built on the same principle. There will be many times when I give of myself; my knowledge and experiences; and my recollections. But there will be times when you will need to give too. You need to do this by getting yourself a DBT diary. This can be an online document or an old-school journal to capture your thoughts. I promise to never ask you to start an entry in this journal with the old clichéd words, "Dear Diary…," but you need to promise to complete the writing assignments I do give, as there went a lot of thought into each of these to ensure you reap optimal benefits from reading this book. I want you to see concrete changes in your life and be able to effectively manage your anger when we go our separate ways.

In your DBT journal, reflect on an instance where you've been unforgiving in expressing your anger. Don't summarize the event; rather, expand on the details of what happened before you were triggered, what the trigger was, what thoughts went through your mind, how you blew off steam, the collateral damage you've caused, and that sinking feeling of regret you've felt afterward. Sit with your anger for a while. Nobody has ever conquered anything by running away from it, and now is the time to face your anger.

But I want you to go deeper too. While you are capturing your story, I want you to constantly ask yourself why you act in this manner and respond as you did. I want you to delve into the underlying emotions that surfaced as anger. By dissecting your anger, you'll get familiar with it, and this familiarity is the starting point of our journey. Enjoy the process.

CHAPTER 2: INTRODUCING MINDFULNESS

66 Mindfully recognizing being overwhelmed already
reduces the feeling of being overwhelmed 99

— *Lilian Cheung*

So, what is DBT, or dialectical behavior therapy? Maybe you've already made the connection between the word dialectical and talking. If this is the case, you likely assume that the therapy has something to do with using speech to change behavior. If so, then you are almost spot on. DBT is a type of talk therapy to help ease the intensity with which you experience emotions. While it has initially been used as a type of therapy to address several major psychological concerns—like post-traumatic stress disorder (PTSD), borderline personality disorder (BPD), suicidal behavior, self-harm, and even depression and anxiety—the benefit of this type of therapy quickly became evident to address other concerns too.

We can say that DBT is a leg of another type of therapy: cognitive behavioral therapy (CBT). CBT specifically focuses on providing those who are experiencing intense emotions with a way to better identify what they are feeling, accept these feelings even when it is tough to do so, learn how to manage these emotions effectively, and then also teach the skills needed to make changes that will benefit your overall well-being.

What sets DBT apart from CBT is that in CBT, you'll learn how to change your current habits and beliefs, or, simply put, your known ways to improve how you think and consequently behave. DBT takes this one step further, a step many consider contradictory. DBT does all the above mentioned as part of CBT, but it also teaches the necessary skills to accept yourself for who you are. So, here you'll learn both acceptance of the self and the skills to change the self to become more of the person you want to be. This is vital, so let's pause for a moment. I hear you ask how I accept myself as I am and change myself simultaneously, and your question is entirely valid.

Whether you are cooking a meal from a recipe or solving a problem as part of a math or science assignment, you first need to understand and grasp the content you are working with before you can make any improvements. Similarly, you first need to understand yourself—something that truly only happens once you've gained an appreciation for who you are—to be able to make any changes.

Let's make this more practical and assume you need to be more carefree. You sometimes find yourself looking at your peers and thinking, How can they laugh so freely? Why don't they feel as pressured as I do? Why are they so confident in who they are? Why does everyone else seem to have a load of fun all the time, and I just don't? Then, the desire to be more carefree begins to rise within. Now, you want to be carefree and may even pretend to be more like the others. Yet, it is not authentic, for you only hold up a front. See, there are times when we can fake it until we make it, but this is not one of those times. To experience the same emotional freedom and joyous contentment you observe in others, you first need to understand why you are not naturally leaning in that direction. You have to understand and accept yourself first. Once you comprehend why you are the way you are, you can work effectively to create the desired outcome. That is, why you must accept yourself comes first, and then learning the tools to be more like you want comes easier.

What will DBT expect of you? Even though it doesn't feel that way, you are the master pulling the puppet strings of your life. You are the only one with the power to change who you are. Based on that knowledge, DBT, or any other type of therapy, will only be as effective in helping you if you are committed to change. Thus, DBT works best if you are amped to change for the positive by applying yourself without reservation to therapy and homework assignments and by shifting your focus from the past to the present moment and future. You'll also benefit from attending group sessions where you can connect with others experiencing similar challenges.

HOW CAN DBT BENEFIT YOU?

Maybe we live in a skeptical world, or maybe we don't, but I've also been an angry teenager not too long ago. I know that skepticism easily becomes the tool we use to keep ourselves from getting pulled into matters demanding stepping outside our comfort zones. So, I want you to be skeptical, for once you've got the answers you are looking for, your level of commitment to DBT will be much higher.

The best place to start is to explore what DBT looks like. At the core of DBT and what sets it apart from other forms of therapy is that it focuses on methods to find a balance between accepting oneself and changing who you are. This is achieved by teaching skills, making both desired treatment outcomes possible.

DBT can be presented as individual therapy sessions, group sessions, consultations, phone coaching, or skills training classes. While your journey with DBT doesn't have to include all these alleys toward success, it will likely consist of more than one route to achieving your desired success.

As DBT has already early on shown immensely positive results as a medium to resolve several concerns teenagers are dealing with, it has been adapted to address particular concerns surfacing during this developmental stage of life. The most noticeable difference between DBT for adults and teenagers is that the adapted version for teenagers focuses on including parents or other caregivers—even family sessions aren't uncommon in this approach. Soon, professionals in the field realized that through the involvement of caregivers, the results achieved by the form of therapy turned out to be much more effective.

Now that you have a better idea of how DBT is presented, we can move on to exploring the techniques used. The type of therapy mainly centers around several methods:

Validation: It teaches how to validate feelings. I would describe this as the basis of DBT, as it is essential to learning the skills needed to understand and validate your feelings and those of others. Even when you are wrapped in conflict, it remains vital to honor the emotions, thoughts, and actions you bring to the conversation and those of the other person, regardless of who they are.

Behavioral change: Once validation takes place, it is easier to change behavior. However, it is not only a case of behavior that needs to change. These changes should also take place in such a manner that it is sustainable. Change without sustainability is futile.

Conversation: Another component of validation is that it requires a conversation that flows from both opposing sides. It means you must verbally express your thoughts and feelings and offer the other person the opportunity to do the same.

Acceptance: This becomes much easier when you accept yourself for who you are. This is where mindfulness comes in as a critical component of the process, as greater self-awareness is achieved through mindfulness.

Mindfulness: The term mindfulness is often confusing to those who have never been introduced to the concept. Mindfulness doesn't come naturally in the world we are living in, as we are mostly surrounded by a busy environment aiming to attract our attention. When we allow any other force to consume our minds, we lose focus on what we are feeling, hearing, experiencing, or even seeing in the present moment. Social media and the constant influx of information through excessive online time are some of the most known forces distracting our attention. Yet, it also happens while walking in the streets of our neighborhoods, cities, or even in the passages at school where there is an overstimulation of the senses. We live in an age where there are so many outside forces for which sustainability depends on how well it can attract our attention and get our buy-in to what it offers. It steals our focus, robs our time, and prevents living and experiencing the present moment.

How does all of this happen? Let me give you a practical example of how these forces rob you of the opportunity to be mindful. Think back to when you were having a snack or meal at your computer or browsing on your phone. Whether interacting on social media or chats, or watching a movie, a favored series, or just clips, your mind was consumed with what was happening on the screen.

Were you able to taste the food you were eating? You may have finished a plate without ever noticing the texture of the food. It is when we can go through an entire bag of chips without ever taking notice of the flavor, the crunch between our teeth, or the salty taste it has. When it happens, you know that you were robbed of being mindful.

Mindfulness demands that you slow down, shift your focus to the present moment, and simply experience every stimulus from your current environment. It means that when you eat, you notice the flavors and colors of your food and the texture it has in your mouth. When you are walking to school, feel the wind on your cheeks and notice the new green growth on the trees marking the start of a different season. Or, when you shower, feel the warm sensation of the water on your skin or the smooth, soapy lather of your shampoo or soap.

When you've accomplished a greater proficiency in all these skills and techniques, you'll be able to find the golden midway. Wandering on the middle path means seeing both sides of the story. It helps you change your behavior to encourage a mutually beneficial outcome during conflict situations instead of showing destructive anger. This is how you develop your personal skills to validate your feelings and emphasize those of another.

When this happens, you essentially overcome your anger and take control of your thoughts, behavior, and, consequently, your life. It is when you become capable of putting yourself in someone else's shoes without feeling that you are giving up some of yourself in the process; when you can grow a greater understanding of why your parents or school have specific rules in place, keeping you from doing certain things; also, when you can allow others to have a particular opinion that differs from yours without feeling the need to convince them otherwise with the force of your anger. Walking on the middle path also gives you the insight to forgive others for hurting you. This forgiveness is not saying that it is okay and that they can just get away with what they did; rather, it is okay as your feelings are validated, and you choose to no longer carry the burden of anger and resentment they caused you to feel. Walking the middle path is the journey to much greater emotional freedom and more effective management of your emotions.

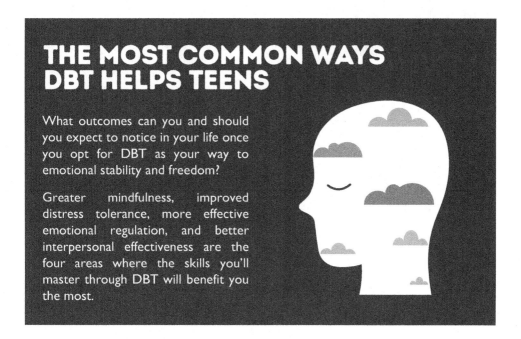

THE MOST COMMON WAYS DBT HELPS TEENS

What outcomes can you and should you expect to notice in your life once you opt for DBT as your way to emotional stability and freedom?

Greater mindfulness, improved distress tolerance, more effective emotional regulation, and better interpersonal effectiveness are the four areas where the skills you'll master through DBT will benefit you the most.

MINDFULNESS

When you are more mindful, you'll notice that your emotions are things you experience, not who you are. You may feel sadness, but it doesn't mean you are a sad person. You may feel anger, but it doesn't mean you are an angry person. Emotions are fleeting and something we experience, but they don't define who we are.

When you are more mindful, you'll enjoy a greater awareness of the feelings that pass through you and become better at letting whatever you feel flow through without holding onto these feelings and assuming them to be part of your identity.

I remember it was an exhilarating, freeing moment when I realized that although I may feel anger in that specific moment, rejection, disappointment, or any other emotion, I don't need to hang onto these emotions. They are just something I feel, and the feeling will pass soon.

Other added benefits to being more mindful include improved focus; you'll get better at memorizing information and notice a reduction in your stress and anxiety levels. Mindfulness also does wonders to relieve the symptoms of depression (Cherry, 2022).

DISTRESS TOLERANCE

We all go through tough moments from time to time. While being in the middle of such a challenging time in your life—it may be a tricky subject at school, being socially rejected, the divorce of your parents, the death of a beloved grandparent, or maybe even a romantic breakup—you are often bombarded with two sets of negative emotions.

The first set is a healthy reflection of what you are feeling; hurt, rejection, disappointment, sadness, or any other feelings the situation may stir. The second set of negative emotions is less promising. These are the negative emotions you feel because you must endure challenging times.

Ready for an example? Sandra's parents are getting a divorce. They waited for her 16th birthday party to happen, and 2 days later, they told her that they were splitting up and that she, her younger brother, and their mom would be staying behind in the family home while her father moves into an apartment in the city at the end of the month. Sandra is sad, shocked, concerned, and already missing her dad, even though there are 10 more days before he leaves. These are all natural emotions to feel, and gradually, Sandra will work through them. While experiencing these negative emotions, Sandra also feels sorry for her parents. She knows that they must have pondered on this decision for quite some time before making their final choice and that, even then, they held back on breaking their sad news until after her birthday, careful not to spoil the magical moment for her.

Now, we have a different version of Sandra's life. She is still in the same position but deals with more negative emotions. She feels that it is unfair that this is happening to her. Sandra accuses her parents of being selfish and not considering her feelings. She mostly walks around angry at home, as she feels that her parents are wrong and messed up by allowing their marriage to fail and that now she has to pay the price for their mistakes. Sandra considers herself to be the victim of her parents' divorce.

Can you see that Sandra's entire outlook on her parents' divorce doesn't consider their feelings in the second scenario? That she doesn't even recognize that they, too, are going through a difficult time and that she is selfishly making it all about her? Therefore, she'll want to punish everyone with her anger.

In the second scenario, Sandra lacks distress tolerance; in the first scenario, her behavior reflects that of someone who can empathize and manage her distress well. In the first version, Sandra can effectively work through her emotions and find healing for the hurt her parents' divorce is causing in her life without making it harder for them and her little brother. In the second, Sandra is not addressing her actual emotions, as every emotion she experiences is overcast by her anger, anger that also makes the situation much worse for her parents and sibling. Can you see how greater distress tolerance can make a vast difference in your life and your relationships? There is a saying that the problem is not the problem—the way we see the problem is the problem.

EMOTIONAL REGULATION

Do you tend to lash out at others when you are tired or stressed? Do you avoid social interaction when you suffer humiliation? It can happen that you've developed a go-to response for every situation in your life, and this response may not necessarily be the most effective approach nor the one that will even resolve the emotions you are experiencing. DBT teaches the needed skills to acknowledge feelings for what they are and the skills to address each emotion most appropriately and effectively.

Through DBT, you'll also learn how to shift your focus from every situation's negative aspects to see the positive in every event. Even from what you perceive as the worst scenario, good can come—you only need to know how to see these positives. I'll be the first to admit that seeing the positive can be challenging when disaster strikes, but there is always some good in every situation.

Can you recall any past events that you've felt were the worst that could happen to you, but now that time has passed, you can see that there were also positive things that resulted from the situation?

INTERPERSONAL EFFECTIVENESS

How well do you rate your ability to maintain your relationships? Interpersonal effectiveness is linked to the ability to manage your emotions and expectations within a relationship with those of another (Cherry, 2022). It is the foundation of strong bonds. You are bound to have stronger, happier, and healthier relationships by improving this skill.

Keith and Megan had been dating for a couple of months when it was time for his prom. As Megan was a year younger than Keith, she knew that while she had specific ideas about what she wanted to look like when going to the dance, this was Keith's moment to shine. Therefore, she didn't expect the focus to be on her. While dressing in vintage clothes was not her preferred choice, she decided to hold on to the dress she dreamed about for her prom the following year and opted for a dress that complimented Keith's vintage outfit. As long as he has fun at his prom, she'll be happy too—she just wants to enjoy the time with him and make some beautiful memories. It is how she showed interpersonal effectiveness by balancing her needs with those of Keith.

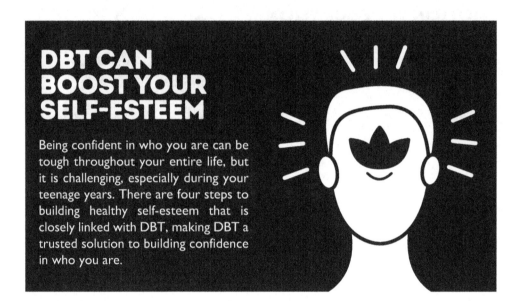

DBT CAN BOOST YOUR SELF-ESTEEM

Being confident in who you are can be tough throughout your entire life, but it is challenging, especially during your teenage years. There are four steps to building healthy self-esteem that is closely linked with DBT, making DBT a trusted solution to building confidence in who you are.

BE FAIR

DBT encourages a fair approach to all in life. Being fair can contribute hugely towards your relationships as it will keep you from shifting blame or judging others. Being fair also demands that you are kind to yourself by not putting your needs and desires on the back burner all the time.

Yes, there will be times when being fair asks you to give someone else's needs preference above yours, but this shouldn't be the case the entire time. Fairness means that you can always be sure that you are doing the right thing, even when it is not pleasant.

DON'T OVER-APOLOGIZE

The therapy teaches that there is a time and a place to apologize in life but never over-apologize. Never feel the need to apologize for saying no. It may be that you want to soften the blow when you do say no, but this may only lead to a buildup of resentment that transforms into excessive anger again. This is a lesson that Buddy had to learn the hard way.

He couldn't wait for the new year to start as he was so keen to join the drama club at his new school. Buddy saw himself on the stages of the world and wanted to start his career right away. When school started, his friend Jimmy asked him to join the swimming team as Jimmy didn't have the confidence to go to the swimming club alone. First, Buddy said, "Sorry, Jimmy, I just can't. Drama and swimming are meeting at the same time, and if I go with you, I won't be able to be part of the drama club."

However, while Jimmy didn't have the confidence to go swimming on his own, he did know how to be persistent until Buddy changed his mind. Initially, Buddy tried to pretend he liked it, but gradually it became more evident that he regretted his mistake. One day, while walking home, Jimmy made a silly joke, and it caused Buddy to respond in anger. All the resentment he felt towards Jimmy for choosing Jimmy over his dreams erupted in a rage that Buddy had no control over. Buddy didn't go back to swimming. He also didn't join the drama club. The two were no longer friends.

Buddy shouldn't have felt bad over his choice to pick his dreams. He wouldn't have robbed Jimmy of anything if he did, but his failure to say no cost him a lot.

DETERMINE & CELEBRATE YOUR VALUES

Self-esteem and values are also two concepts that are closely linked. DBT helps in this regard, as it encourages you to identify your values. These values will determine every choice you make in the future. The stronger you are set in your values, the more likely you are to stick to them. Each time you choose to act in line with your values, your self-esteem expands, turning you into the confident person you want to be.

When you are confident in who you are, it becomes much easier to accept that anger is something you feel, not who you are. When you've grasped that, dealing with your anger—and all other emotions—becomes much easier.

DIGGING DEEPER

It is time again to grab your DBT journal.

At the core of DBT, we'll find mindfulness. It is the essential first step you need to take to identify your emotions; to create distance between what you feel and who you are; and to define your values. The concept of mindfulness can often sound more daunting than it is. You can practice mindfulness throughout the day, wherever you go, but before you can do so on your way to school, while taking your shower, or during any meal, you need to experience what it entails. Now is that moment.

I want you to find a place to sit without being disturbed. If you can find such a spot somewhere in nature, it would be even better.

Find a comfortable position and take a few deep breaths. Then, without thinking, write in your DBT journal what you are feeling, smelling, seeing, and hearing—are you sitting on a lawn, perhaps? Then, write how the grass touching your legs feels—is the air hot, humid, cold, chilly, or soothing? Are there any strong-smelling flowers around you? Do you hear laughter, the conversations of others perhaps? Now, if you listen more attentively, do you hear birds, insects, or the buzzing city in the background? How do all these things make you feel? Are you feeling content, happy, nervous, excited, or relaxed?

It doesn't matter how long it takes you; be sure to capture every detail of the moment. Pin down your external experiences and your internal realizations. During this time you've spent being aware of your surroundings, you've been mindful, you employed greater awareness, and were living in the present moment. The more you practice mindfulness, the more it will become your way of living. Are you ready to observe the world with different eyes? Start doing so today.

CHAPTER 3:
THE BEGINNING OF CHANGE

66
No one heals himself by wounding another
99

— *Ambrose*

You know it, and I know it. After going through the motions of experiencing extreme rage, after the hurtful outburst of anger, there is no healing. You don't feel any better than before. Sure, you feel less tense since you've let off some steam, but in most cases, steam is just hot air that burns those who come too close to it. Steam doesn't heal your hurt; it only hurts another. The moment it is all over, the regret and shame for your behavior kick in almost instantly. The self-castigation starts, and so does the buildup leading to your next explosive expression of anger. You are the only one capable of putting an end to this vicious cycle. Only you can choose to take control of your anger and emotions. Only you can stop hurting those around you.

Are you ready to learn the required skills for expressing your anger healthily and constructively rather than leaving a trail of destruction as far as you go?

HEALTHY WAYS TO EXPRESS ANGER EFFECTIVELY AND MEANINGFULLY

For the longest time, I thought the way we express anger was the same for everyone and that there is only one way to show that you are angry. I just assumed those around me who didn't express anger in the manner I did were just not ever as angry as I was. Maybe they just didn't ever have any reason to show anger.

DBT helped me to realize that I was completely wrong for most of my life. Through therapy, I realized that there are ways to show your anger that can be less hurtful, even productive and good, if you use healthy techniques.

After all that I've learned about anger and how to effectively manage my rage, the solution I came up with was to create and establish my "anger response plan." You are most likely familiar with an evacuation plan. Every school should have one, and if school management is diligent in keeping safety protocols, you've likely been part of several evacuation plan simulations or drills. Some kids in my school considered these drills a nuisance as they meant that they had to get up and leave the school building. However, others, including myself, liked these drills as they ate into the time we had to spend in class. I also felt that fire drills gave an exciting twist to the day. It is probably also why the idea of having a similar plan in place to address anger was so attractive to me. The core purpose of a fire drill is to minimize injury and to ensure that in the case of an actual emergency, everyone is clear on what to do to reduce the risk of injury, fatalities, and damage to property. Once the alarm triggers a response—and the alarm can go off at any time—the immediate response simply kicks into gear without thinking about what to do next.

CREATING AN ANGER RESPONSE PLAN

I am sharing the steps of my anger response plan as it includes several helpful techniques and steps to express your anger more effectively and to help you to maintain control over your emotions and behavior.

BE ALERT TO THE SIGNS

The sound of an alarm is the trigger to respond during a fire drill. When it comes to anger, the signals you'll receive may be more subtle than the shrill sound of your school's fire alarm. Yet, as you become more mindful of your emotions and the sensations you experience throughout the day, you'll get better at recognizing them long before you crash and burn.

The common signs of a rise in anger are your heart racing, feeling shaky, or your tone of voice may change when you talk, becoming higher and shriller. Others may grind their teeth, start pacing around, feel hot, as well as be more critical, judgmental, and snappy. In most cases, if you usually have a great sense of humor, your sense of finding things funny will dissipate.

DETERMINE THE ROOT OF YOUR ANGER

Now, you are alerted to the state you are in, and it is time to determine from where the cause of concern is originating. The sooner the fire can be located, the sooner you can extinguish the flames before it turns into a fierce rage. So, ask yourself, what is making you angry? Maybe you are hungry, tired, overwhelmed by conditions beyond your control, hurt, disappointed, going through hormonal changes, feeling rejected or left out, or any other reason you can think of that is not sitting well in your mind.

I've found that writing down my thoughts helps a lot to get to the root of my concerns if I struggle to determine the exact cause of what is fueling this anger inside me. Mostly, I write in my journal—similar to your DBT journal—but there have been times when I captured my emotions in a letter. Then I can directly express my feelings towards the person I've identified as the one causing me to feel this inner strife. DO NOT SEND THE LETTER, though—at least, not the first draft. During the first draft of such a letter, you are likely still ranting and blowing off steam in an out-of-control manner. Once you finish the letter, get up and go for a walk. Come back and reread it with a perspective of how you can say what you want to say more nicely. Maybe you feel that you don't have to send any letters at all anymore. That is good. If you still feel the need to get your word out, then start from scratch and capture your emotions again without the anger you've already let go of in the first draft.

COUNTING, COUNTING, & MORE COUNTING

Are you familiar with the advice of counting to 10 when you are angry? I've concluded that counting to 10 is useless for me. What helps me is to count to 100. Yet, it is not only about thinking about the counting but to think about something that doesn't upset me for 100 seconds.

So, set your timer for 100 seconds—that would be 1 minute and 40 seconds—and while the timer is ticking, think only about something you enjoy. It can be a book, a movie, a person who makes you laugh a lot, a funny joke you've heard, or anything else. Avoid cheating, as by doing so, you are only cheating yourself. Repeat the 100 seconds until you've managed to think for 100 seconds only about something pleasant. I promise your anger will be much more manageable once you are done.

TAKE A TIMEOUT

There is nothing wrong with taking a timeout when you need it. Whenever you feel more signals alerting you of the rise of anger internally while being in a conversation or even within a particular situation, take a timeout. Excuse yourself and put the distance you need between yourself and the cause of your anger.

Use this timeout to take a couple of deep breaths in a neutral environment. Get active and go for a quick walk around the school, jog in your neighborhood, or maybe take the family dog for a walk. Physical activity and time in nature have a soothing effect on emotions. Once you are ready, you can approach the conversation or situation again; as you'll be much calmer now, you'll remain in better control of the emotions stirred inside.

SOOTHE YOURSELF

We never know when the emergency alarm is going to rip through the present moment with a shrill sound. However, I've learned that by being more mindful and aware of what I am feeling, I can take certain steps to increase my overall calmness:

I listen to music. When I was younger—much younger—the sounds blasting from my stereo were quite angry. Now I know better; this type of music isn't an expression of my anger; it only increases the anger that I am already feeling. Since I've switched to listening to calmer tones, I can feel my anger melting away. I am not saying you need to listen to Simon and Garfunkel or perhaps a few sonatas—not that there's anything wrong with these, and I love them too—but go for the milder side of your music collection to calm your mood.

Practicing gratitude has also helped me a great deal, and therefore, I still hold onto this routine. I've established a habit of writing one thing that I am grateful for on a piece of paper, and then I fold the note and chuck it into a large jar that I keep on my nightstand. Whenever I feel that my anger is rising, I go to my jar and read some of the notes I wrote. When I remind myself again of all the good that I have in my life, anger usually comes in second.

Finding a creative outlet for my anger has also panned out well. The added benefit is that I have several interesting sculptures in my home that serve both as reminders to myself that my anger doesn't have to control me and as a dramatic touch to my décor. Whether it is songwriting, painting, sketching, or like in my case, sculpting that speaks to you, rely on your creativity to positively channel your energy.

DRILL IN YOUR ACTION PLAN

This brings me to a second benefit of having my sculptures to mind. They serve as reminders that I am capable of managing my anger. I compare them to the evacuation plans that you'll see in large apartment blocks, hotels, resorts, and your school, to name only a few locations, where these plans are visible to all to see. Even if you've never been part of an emergency drill in these buildings, walking past these plans serves as a reminder that there is a way out of every bad situation—you just need to stick to your plans. Find a format that you are comfortable with to remind you that you too have a plan in place to get you out of the sticky situation of being angry while preventing any injury.

THE PROS & CONS OF ANGER

I've touched now several times already on using anger constructively or effectively, but let's put the positive use of anger under the microscope to see what the pros and cons are that the emotion brings about.

THE CONS OF ANGER

It almost feels like I want to ask you what you want first: the bad news or the not-so-bad news? Quite simply, I've experienced that for every so-called "pro" to the expression of anger, you can establish the same results, or even better, by following a different approach than one fueled by an underlying rage. Yet, let's start with the bad news before moving on to the not-so-bad, right?

As you are more than likely already very familiar with the cons of anger, I think merely listing them will suffice. You are, of course, also welcome to add more of the cons you've experienced in your life:

✓ Anger is bad for your health. It increases your blood pressure and heart rate and the excess pressure on your cardiac system increases the risk of heart attacks and strokes (Promises Behavioral Health, 2022).

✓ It crushes your relationships.

✓ Our anger outbursts impact the way others see you; they lose respect for you and become weary of being around you.

✓ These outbursts and their severity tend to cause you humiliation and feelings of regret over what you've done or said. These feelings have a negative ripple effect on your self-esteem and confidence.

✓ Anger leaves you feeling on the edge all the time.

✓ It robs you of experiencing joy; laughter and fun; opportunities; and meaningful bonds.

✓ When anger is extremely out of control, it can get you a criminal record, resulting in costly settlements.

✓ While being blinded by your anger, you can cause irreversible harm that you have to live with for the rest of your life.

✓ Anger increases feelings of isolation, anxiety, stress, and the possibility of depression ("What Is Anger?" n.d.).

What other cons can you add to the list?

THE NOT-SO-BAD NEWS

To be fair, there can come some good from anger too. Anger is such a potent emotion, loaded with energy, that it can give you the boost to act on what you've been procrastinating on for far too long. Therefore, anger is also helpful for instigating change. For example, certain social atrocities may go unnoticed by those in power and are able to bring about change until the anger of the masses evolves into protests which then shed the essential light on the concerns to bring change:

> Anger may get you to take up an exercise routine; clean your house or room; and start ticking things off your to-do list that becomes very lengthy as time passes.

> It also gives you the courage to speak up when you might have shied away from a topic or person for too long.

> You discharge emotionally.

> Your anger can lead to the punishment of those who did you wrong.

> Anger tends to get you attention, but is it the kind of attention you desire?

You may have a few points you want to add to the list too. Yet, you could've achieved all of the above without putting your mind and body through the impact anger has on it and without taking the risk of facing potentially dire consequences. There are far more productive and wholesome ways to achieve all of the above positive outcomes of anger. It is why I am not so much in support of using a high-risk emotion as a tool to establish any desired result.

RESPONDING VS. REACTING

Have you received this advice in the past and thought what does it even mean? Aren't the two terms synonyms? I remember my confusion about what I was being told the first time I was instructed to respond instead of reacting. I remember the situation so well even though it happened more than 10 years ago already.

I think the reason why this memory stuck so much with me is that I can't believe that I treated my family, the people who love me deeply, so badly.

I was about 16 and couldn't wait for the upcoming summer break. I was tired of being on the edge the entire time, hated school, and just had a massive fallout with a friend. While it sounded super uncool to go with your family on holiday, I knew that when we are on holiday, my parents are way less on my case, meaning there was far more freedom in my life. My mom's family had a cabin at a lake and we would join them. As it was such a small community living in that area, it was quite safe to move around freely, and nobody minded if I would be out the entire day swimming or simply reading while sitting under a tree. I remember how we would sometimes stroll in the streets even after dark, as it was so safe there. So, I was holding on to the idea of breaking free from the norm to get me through the last couple of days of school.

 Then the news broke. My dad's mom had a stroke, and suddenly we were heading toward the opposite side of the state for the entire holiday. He was an only child and his dad passed away a few years before, so he wanted to be there with his mom to care for her when she went home from the hospital.

I hated the town she stayed in. She was very old and her house was stuffy, and I always felt that she didn't like me much. My immediate reaction to this disappointment was to be angry. I felt like the entire world was out to get me and that nobody cared, and I wasn't going to tolerate this treatment anymore. I was horrible. Instead of being there for my dad—and my mom—I made everyone's lives miserable. Nobody could talk to me without me biting off their heads. One day, my anger erupted so badly, I slammed a door after losing my voice while screaming at my parents, and I knocked over a crystal vase that belonged to my gran, the gran who was dying. I'll never forget the expression on my dad's face when I looked up from the shattered pieces on the floor. I wanted to clean it up and he just told me to go. I remember feeling sorry, guilty, lonely, isolated, and hurt at the same time—it was horrible. My parents decided to take me to my family at the lake house and they went to my other gran. She passed away a few days later without me seeing her or ever saying goodbye. The irony is that after all the hurt and heartache, my parents still spend most of the holidays at the lake house, but there was this awkward thing between me & my dad, a thing that took years before it finally got resolved.

It could've been different if I only responded rather than reacted.

The difference between reacting and responding to a situation is that reacting happens rapidly. We are exposed to a trigger and, without delay, we react. We don't allow time for the mud to settle, for emotions to calm down, or for clear thinking to return to the surface.

Responding is different. When we respond, we wait before saying or doing anything. We hold onto what we want to say to see if our words or the way we express ourselves will improve. It requires delayed action.

The process of reacting can be dissected into three steps: stimulus, anger, and action.

Responding consists of more processes. Here, we have a stimulus, anger, a pause to process, and we plan a response—only then does the action take place.

Knowing what I know now, I can see how the situation with my grandma could've been entirely different. Yes, I was tired and deserved a break. However, there was no way that my parents would've known what would happen to my dad's mother. For him to want to go to be by her side was only normal, and of course, my mom would also want to be there to support him and her mother-in-law—I mean, it was only the right thing to do. If I would've given the time needed to respond, I could've supported my parents too, and still considered the time away from the norm as a break. I could've understood that they were tired, stressed, and concerned too; that my dad was sad and probably also felt some regrets for not being there immediately when his mother needed him. I would've realized all of this if I allowed time for the mud to settle and not only think about myself.

DIGGING DEEPER

Are you ready to up the efforts needed to establish change? I have two exercises that will benefit you.

In the first exercise, I want you to create your anger response plan. It would mean that you have to write down the steps you need to follow when the anger alarm is bringing your life to a stop. Have fun while doing so and give this plan any format that speaks to you.

You can make a poster; have a complete outline; write down an action plan; lay out your actions in the form of speech bubbles; add color and images; and claim this plan as yours. The following questions will guide you along the way:

- ✓ What signs register as warnings that an emergency is heading your way?

- ✓ What processes or routines can you put in place to buy yourself the time to determine what is causing you to feel this anger? When this warning signal goes off in a building, the desired response is to leave the building in an orderly manner. So, determine your go-to reaction when you notice these signs.

- ✓ Identify the possible obstacles you may experience along the way and determine how you can overcome these with ease.

- ✓ List several actions you can take to soothe yourself, to give the mud time to settle, and to get logic to overcome emotion so that you can respond rather than react.

✓ Once you are done, place this plan where you'll see if it often—at best, daily. This way, whenever you are getting triggered, you don't have to think about how you want or need to respond; you can simply follow the instructions set out on your anger response plan.

The second task I want you to complete is to remember a time when you reacted. List the cons that resulted from your reaction and ponder if there were any possible cons. Now that you know better, you can do better. So, if you can replay the specific situation, what would you do differently, as you would be responding rather than reacting? Now, list the possible pros and cons of the situation.

When your changed approach to the conflict situation leaves you feeling proud of yourself, then pat yourself on the back. It is time to reward yourself—you may not have noticed it yet, but you've already taken huge steps to improve your behavior and become the master of your emotions.

Maybe you are familiar with Robin Sharma and his bestselling book—the first of a couple more—The Monk Who Sold His Ferrari, or perhaps you've never heard of him. Regardless, he says that things happen twice: first in our minds and then in reality. If you've reached a stage where you can plan and maybe even dream about your changed behavior when angered, you are already halfway there.

The more you think about the person you want to be when you are angry or how you want to respond when you are triggered, the more natural your desired way of managing your anger will become to fulfill the next time when all the pawpaw hits the fan.

CHAPTER 4: MASTERING YOUR BODY

The human body is a complex and intricate network in which the mind, body, and soul all impact each other. Anxiety and stress are often accompanied by a sense of having butterflies in the stomach; similarly, fear can make us shiver, feel nauseous, or have difficulty breathing. These are all examples of how our emotional state can impact us physically. Comparably, anger also manifests physically, and the same happens when we are exposed to anger triggers. I've learned that the physical responses of my body to these triggers often alert me of the fact that I am being triggered. By becoming acquainted with these physical responses, I've found a tool to become alert to what is going to happen if I don't act to change the course in advance. By familiarizing yourself with the most common physical responses of anger triggers, and by identifying the triggers unique to you, you give yourself a little more time to steer the explosive situation in a different—and safer—direction.

UNDERSTANDING THE PHYSICAL MANIFESTATION OF ANGER

Are you up for a quick biology lesson? Anger, like any other emotion, is caused by chemicals released in the brain. These chemicals instruct the body to prepare itself physically for a specific type of situation. The part of the brain responsible for the release of the hormones linked to anger, is the amygdala, a small part of the brain shaped like two almonds.

Once the body senses a situation that might be a threat, the amygdala responds by releasing hormones that prepare the body to fight. Part of the preparation includes releasing hormones giving the body an energy burst that will last for up to a few minutes. While the entire process I've described here can happen within the wink of an eye, after the energy has been released, it can take much longer until your body returns to a calm state ("Physiology of Anger," n.d.).

It is due to this process—the release of chemicals—that anger and every other feeling surpass the emotional aspects of our being and also affect us physically.

RECOGNIZING THESE PHYSICAL RESPONSES EARLY ON

Sometimes, it can be hard to determine exactly what you are feeling, judging purely on your emotions alone. However, through mindfulness and by employing greater awareness of the sensations in your body, actions, and any changes in your behavior, you can gather much quicker when anger is rising inside.

I've touched on these physical changes in the previous chapter, but as there is more to say, let's linger on this for a moment.

Anger often manifests in the following manners, but it doesn't mean that it will happen exactly the same for you. Therefore, you need to rely on awareness of physical sensations to become familiar with how your anger triggers manifest physically:

A clenching jaw can be caused by muscles that are pulling tighter and are ready for action.	As digestion is not a physical process necessary to protect yourself in a state of fear, the stress hormones will slow down the circulation to your digestive system to allow greater blood flow to your muscles, bringing them the oxygen they need to fight. As a result, you may experience stomach cramps and aches.	The increased need for oxygen in your muscles demands that your heart rate speeds up to increase circulation. So, it is normal to experience an increased heart rate. By having your heart rate speed up, the blood in your veins is under more pressure, causing an increase in blood pressure that may lead to a headache.	Higher blood pressure is also causing you to feel flushed and sweaty, trembling and shaky. As there is suddenly such a spike in heart rate and blood pressure, it is normal to feel dizzy or light-headed.

While these are the most common ways which anger manifests physically, you are likely to experience several other emotions too. If you are not familiar with identifying the emotions you are experiencing, it is easy to get confused in the heat of the moment and—instead of recognizing the irritation, resentment, anxiety, sadness, guilt, or any other emotion for what it is—to just consider it as anger, leaving you to feel like the anger you are dealing with is much greater than in reality.

These changes also impact your behavior and the following are common behavior changes related to exposure to anger triggers:

You may be cupping your fist with your other hand, indicating you are ready to fight.

You may reach for alcohol or nicotine to "calm your nerves" or to "relax."

Excessive rubbing of the head, especially the forehead, is another sign.

Changes in your tone of voice include a shrill tone or speaking louder, even screaming & shouting.

HOW TO USE STOP EFFECTIVELY

STOP is one of the many skills and techniques I've learned in DBT. As it showed to be a very effective approach to overcoming anger, I've practiced it so often that it has become second nature for me.

Essentially, STOP sums up action steps—or inaction steps—that will help you to respond and not react. STOP is designed in such a manner that it gives time to let the mud settle and for reasoning to surface. Let's break it down:

Stop: Yes, the first action you need to take according to STOP is to stop yourself from reacting toward any of the physical, emotional, or behavioral changes you've noticed. Example time: Let's say your friend blows you off at the last minute when you had plans to go to a party together.

For the entire week, you've been looking forward to it, and you and your best buddy decided to go together as you both had bad breakups this year and decided to go solo for a while. Then the night before the event, you get a text simply stating, "Sorry dude. You're on your own. I'm taking Shelley."

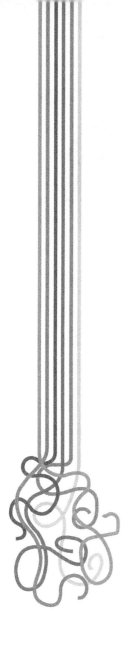

✔ Of course, you are upset. There is no way how you'll find a date before then and you are not going on your own. You are furious and have a selection of words to tell him how much his behavior sucks. Stop!

✔ The best way I can describe it is instead of jumping right onto the matter by sending a text, visualize yourself freezing for a moment.

Take a step back: In your vision, when you unfreeze, take a step back. Your momentum is broken and nothing is propelling you forward anymore. You can take a step back from the trigger to reconsider your position in the situation. Take a few deep breaths and maybe ask yourself if you would've done the same to him if it was you. After all, Shelly is both extremely pretty and super nice. Would you have said no to that? Don't you want your friend—best friend—to be happy after going through such a bad breakup, a pain you've experienced yourself firsthand?

Observe: Now, it is time to shift your focus internally by taking stock of the emotions you are experiencing. So, we know you are disappointed because you don't see how you can go to the party alone. You are angry because your friend chose a girl above you. You think you might have made the same choice and would like him to understand your situation. You are happy for him to get this nice girl to go to the party with him. You are curious as you wonder how it all happened since you saw him at school.

✔ This can indeed be a confusing stage in the process. But, ask yourself what you would recommend someone in your position to do if you were an onlooker on it all. Say, what happened to you, happened to a friend, what would you say to that person and how do you think they should deal with the situation?

Proceed Mindfully: Now you have your answer and know what to do. The initial emotions you've experienced are no longer so intense and you can think clearly and logically about the situation. So, you text him back, "What??? How did that happen? Happy for you dude. Check you anyway at the party. Say hi to Shelley."

Practice this technique as much as possible and see how most of the most intense emotions you experience—that usually cause outrage—dissipate naturally when you decide to STOP rather than act.

HOW TO USE DBT DISTRESS TOLERANCE SKILLS

The STOP skill is one of a larger collection of distress tolerance skills aiming to provide immediate relief to the symptoms you are experiencing at the moment when your anger is highly explosive. These skills are all designed in a manner to help you to accept the reality of your situation with greater ease and to reduce the chances of you taking any impulsive actions you'll most likely regret later on.

By familiarizing myself with these distress-tolerance skills, I could see how it was often my inability to accept the situation that was at the root of my anger explosions—it is with shame that I remind you of my story about how I didn't support my dad at all when his mom had a stroke). These skills can help you to escape any suffering you may experience, caused by your lack of acceptance.

TIPP Like STOP, TIPP is also an acronym for temperature, intense exercise, paced breathing, and paired muscle relaxation.

Visualize yourself being right on the edge of an anger explosion. You are standing on an edge of a volcano, and the moment you lean slightly forward, you'll fall, activating an eruption of hot melted rock that will fly up high into the sky and cause destruction wherever it lands. What are you going to do? Fall forward, or use TIPP to take you in a different direction to defuse the situation, sparing people and places you surround yourself with?

Temperature: The term "hot-headed" came into existence for a reason. While in a state of extreme anger, you are most likely having increased blood circulation to your head, leaving your face feeling warm and red. By cooling yourself down physically, you can calm your mood too. One such way is by going to the bathroom and splashing your face with cold water to ease your emotions.

Intense exercise: As anger is such a potent emotion, you need to discharge the level of energy gathered inside. The most effective way to do this is through exercise that requires as much energy as what you have to give. Sprinting, boxing, jumping jacks, or getting into the pool to swim a couple of laps will all help you to release this energy & decrease your internal pressure without the need to blow your top.

Paced breathing: I've said that the mind and the body are complexly connected and that one has an impact on the other. As stress hormones in your brain can cause your breathing to become shallow and rapid, you use your breathing to reverse this state. Stand upright and place your hands on your belly and then close your eyes and focus on nothing except breathing deeply. Notice how the air passes through your airways and how it fills your lungs, causing your belly to lift your hands. As you exhale, the opposite effect occurs. By slowing your breathing, you reverse the release of stress hormones, leading you to greater emotional calm.

Paired muscle relaxation: You know the feeling. Everything inside of you feels highly strung. You feel like a violin string, ready to snap. The discomfort, almost pain, is the worst in your neck and shoulder areas. By deliberately tightening your muscles and then letting them relax, you'll gradually feel the stress seep out of your body. The best is to start at one end of your body—let's say your toes, and then stretch your toes and work your way towards your feet, ankles, calves, thighs, buttocks, and back until you get to your head and face. Stretch and let go and feel your muscles ease into greater relaxation, your heart pace returning to normal, and your mood alleviating to where it is safe again at the volcano.

ACCEPTS

Another helpful DBT skill to add to your toolbox for anger management is ACCEPTS, which is an acronym that stands for activities, contributing, comparisons, emotions, pushing away, thoughts, and sensations.

The core purpose of ACCEPTS is to use it in a manner that will distract your mind and free it from obsessing over the cause of your anger.

Let's see how it works:

Activities: Identify several activities as your go-to activities when you feel you need to escape from your thoughts or your mind will explode. For the longest time, my go-to was watching Friends replays. I would immerse myself for hours in the lives of Joey, Rachel, Monica, Phoebe, Chandler, and Ross. For you, it may be your favorite series currently airing on Netflix, or hanging with a friend. A friend recently shared how she would escape from her own thoughts by going horse riding. I can just imagine that it can be quite a thrilling experience effectively taking your mind away from your anger.

Contributing: Volunteering is a fantastic way to overcome your stress and concerns. You don't even have to become a volunteer if you don't feel like it, as your help will be as much appreciated when you help a sibling with their homework, a friend with their assignment, your dad in the garden, or by volunteering your help with the laundry, making the literal and figurative load on your mom's shoulders lighter.

Comparison: If you want to compare yourself, then do so by using a former version of yourself as the benchmark. Compare how well you are handling your anger now in relation to a previous event, or compare how much your life improved over the past couple of months.

Emotions: There are several things you can do to change the most predominant emotion you may be experiencing. Music is a powerful tool to change our emotional state. Watching a thriller, scary movie, or comedy will also help to change your mood. I've always been a sucker for romcoms and these are still my go-to movies when I need an emotional reset.

Push away: Just for a moment, or maybe a little longer, decide to actively push away everything that is upsetting or angering you. Allow yourself some space between the origin of your anger and yourself. By allowing this space, you'll likely notice how your perspective on matters changes.

Thoughts: Change your thought patterns by thinking about the dialogue in one of your favorite movies, singing the words of a song you like, grabbing the crossword puzzle, or even sudoku printed on the local paper lying on the kitchen table. It doesn't matter what you do, just change your train of thought.

Thoughts: Change your thought patterns by thinking about the dialogue in one of your favorite movies, singing the words of a song you like, grabbing the crossword puzzle, or even sudoku printed on the local paper lying on the kitchen table. It doesn't matter what you do, just change your train of thought.

GROUNDING YOURSELF

Grounding is another helpful approach to discharging yourself. I know there are many people who are sensitive towards textures and they hate walking barefoot on grass. Others just hate walking barefoot at all. I am one of those people who love the sensation of walking barefoot on a soft lawn after a hard and challenging day. The sensation of the cool soft strands of grass immediately discharges my emotions and I feel almost instant relief.

Through greater awareness of the texture of the grass, the sensation it leaves between my toes, and the softness underneath my heels, I become focused on the present moment. This remains my favorite form of grounding.

How does grounding work? The technique helps you to shift your focus to the present moment and to live in the now. The present moment is a space where there is no reason for concern or a place for regret—it just is. Through grounding, you can ease anxiety, depression, stress, and even PTSD symptoms. These techniques effectively lift your mood and contribute to your overall well-being. The best of it all is that they are really fun exercises.

One way to ground yourself is to look around where you are sitting and to notice the objects within arm's reach. Pick these objects up, one after the other, but take your time with every item and feel the texture. How heavy or light, rough or delicate is the item you are holding? What color is it? Is it hard, squeezy, cold, smooth, fluffy, or bendy?

Sniff your favorite scent. Like music, scents are also potent mood changers. Here, you can choose to sniff your favorite perfume or explore a range of aromas. There are usually a bunch of things to sniff in the kitchen, especially when you tackle the spice rack. Vanilla, coffee, cinnamon, mint, basil, thyme, teas… there are so many to name. Focusing on nothing but the scent you are smelling is another outstanding grounding technique.

DIGGING DEEPER

You are smart, intelligent, capable, and highly resourceful, right? You don't need to just do everything I am telling you to do, even though it will help you a great deal in finding the route to inner calmness & excellent anger management.

You can establish grounding techniques that are unique to your personality. As I've explained how walking barefoot on grass does wonders for my soul, but isn't something everyone will do, I want you to determine three go-to grounding techniques that bring you the best results.

It will mean that you may have to do some of your own research to discover more known DBT grounding techniques, or you can recall what are the simple actions that make you feel grounded. You may not have had a name for the technique before nor have known how to refer to the impact it has on your mood, but now you know.
So, list three different grounding techniques that work for you. Name them, describe them, and be sure to include them in your DBT journal.

Then, practice them so that you never have to think about what to do when you are feeling your emotions rise. You simply do what comes naturally to you as you've done this so many times; it becomes your second nature.

> **Next, I'll tell you how to become a master of your mind.**

CHAPTER 5:
IN TUNE WITH YOUR MIND

66
When you know yourself you are empowered.
When you accept yourself you are invincible.
99

— Tina Lifford

It came to me as quite a surprise the first time I learned that DBT identifies three minds in us all. Nonetheless, once I understood the concept, it made so much sense to me and it supported me greatly to become a master of my emotions.

There are three parts to the mind: the rational mind, the emotional mind, and the wise mind. Ideally, you want the wise mind to be the controlling force in your life, but the wise mind can only exist in the presence of the other two. To live a life where you are in control of all three, you need to be more mindful of what is happening in each of these minds individually as well as grasp and understand how these minds impact each other and the outcome you'll get.

The rational mind guides and contains logical thinking and rationale. On the other end of the spectrum, you'll find the emotional mind that is mostly overreacting as it is allowing emotions to take control. The wise mind presents itself where the rational mind and the emotional mind overlap.

> Now, let's dig into this to see what each of these minds looks like and explore the role they play.

THE EMOTIONAL MIND

It is in the emotional mind where the heat leading to an emotional eruption simmers and stews. By all means, there is a place and a purpose for the emotional mind as it is what enables you to empathize with others; it also enables you to show and feel sympathy and to have compassion.

It is in the emotional mind where the heat leading to an emotional eruption simmers and stews. By all means, there is a place and a purpose for the emotional mind as it is what enables you to empathize with others; it also enables you to show and feel sympathy and to have compassion.

I am not saying that emotion is bad. What I am saying is that when there is limited or no control over the emotional mind, it becomes dangerous.

If your emotional mind is the force in charge of your actions, you are likely to be a passionate person, fighting tooth and nail for what you stand for or believe in. But are you effective in getting what you desire?

Felicity is 16 and identifies as an activist. Activism is good. It highlights social atrocities, stands up for the underdog, and restores injustice in the world, often by creating awareness around the issue. Typically, activists would be made up of people who are passionate about a specific cause. Their behavior is fueled by their intense desire to right a wrong. The way they behave is a product of their deep-rooted commitment to the cause.

Felicity was a bit different. Her activism wasn't rooted in her beliefs or passions. No, she found causes to have an excusable explanation for her actions. I remember her mom saying to me that it sometimes feels as if Felicity is looking for a cause just so that she can let go of her emotions while she shielded her behavior with the excuse that she was an activist. I got the feeling that even though she did care to a certain degree about the causes she was adding her voice to, it was more about her emotions that were out of control than the cause itself.

The cause was merely an excuse for her behavior when she stormed into a top-end restaurant immersed in fake blood and having what appeared to be animal intestines draped around her neck as part of her protest against people eating meat. Another incident occurred when she broke into a private lab to free the animals where she believed a huge cosmetic house was running tests on them and that she was going to expose them. Felicity wound up getting arrested for breaking in and trespassing on private property, and it wasn't her first and wouldn't be her last arrest.

The problem was that Felicity wasn't vegan or vegetarian, and she wore makeup from the best-known cosmetic brands too. She merely adapted her activism to find a cause giving her an outlet for her intense emotions. Her emotional brain was dictating her every move and her mother rightfully feared that soon she would take it too far, landing her in hot water.

THE REASONABLE MIND

If the emotional mind is warm andpassionate, the reasonable mind is cold and calculated. When the reasonable mind is in charge, your moves will be precise and controlled—overtly so. To act according to reason is good when present in healthy quantities. For example, say your mom asked you to pick up a few things from the grocery store after school. You have two choices: You can either walk home on the same route you normally do and then go to the grocery store, or you can walk a slightly different route and stop at the grocery store on your way home. The latter is a reasonable choice for it will help you save time and effort.

When the level of reason you showcase becomes so overpowering that it casts a shadow on all you say and do, it is problematic though. Then, others will likely refer to you as cold, heartless, lacking compassion, and hard to connect with. You'll struggle to have any meaningful relationships. It will make it hard for your future coworkers to work with you as you come across as someone who lacks an understanding of what is at the heart of humanity. Yes, sure, you may likely never experience an emotional explosion, but that doesn't mean that these feelings aren't brewing toxically underneath the surface.

His reasonable mind ruled Denver. As it was hard for others to form any connection with him, he would always end up alone during teamwork exercises. If someone was instructed to work with him, his entire class openly pitied that person. Denver was the person who told the principal every time when the janitor slept on the job. He went as far as to take pictures of the sleeping man and threatened to take the matter to the school board if the principal doesn't remove the janitor for his inadequate performance. Yes, the janitor was wrong, but he only slept because his wife was dying of cancer; when she had a bad night, he would be up the entire time to help her be more comfortable with her pain. Denver's complaints eventually resulted in the janitor losing his job. He couldn't afford medicine for his wife anymore, and two weeks later, she passed away.

The entire school was heartbroken for they mostly cared deeply about the man, but Denver persisted that the janitor was wrong and deserved the action taken against him.

Can you see that even if you are ruled by the rational mind and never have an emotional outburst, your action can still be extremely hurtful?

THE WISE MIND

At the sweet spot where rationale and emotion overlap, you find the wise mind. It is a place where balance exists and where intuition has an important role to play. The internal equilibrium creates a welcoming place where the inner voice can be heard. The wise mind can make smart moves resulting from rational thinking and inspired empathy and compassion for others.

It attaches value to gut feelings and seeks deeper meaning in life, events, and relationships. It is the optimal mental space to settle in.

The wise mind is available to all to access and is what elevates your words, behavior, and actions to make a meaningful impact on the world and the lives of others.

> **How will learning the skills to employ the wise mind benefit Felicity & Denver?**

The biggest revelation Felicity couldprobably have is that one attracts more flies with honey than vinegar. If she changed her approach to activism to only stand up for the causes she truly believes in, her efforts to establish change will be fueled by her passion for the cause and not by the desire to cause "meaningful" disruption. As these efforts will also be less diluted, they will be more effective. Say she decided to stick to promoting a meat-free environment as her cause of choice, then her strategy could've changed in the following manner:

> She'll stop eating meat and meat products herself.

> Felicity would commit her time to sharing accurate information about the impact commercial farming has on the environment and the cruelty that is often inherent to commercial farming.

> She would select her target audience to be people who are on the verge of making the transition, rather than disrupting a crowd so badly that they choke on their last bite of a chop or steak.

> She would refrain from actions causing damage to the properties of private people and entities and from disrupting their operations in such a manner that it damages their brand identity.

Denver had to move more toward having an emotional side to his approach:

> Felicity would commit her time to sharing accurate information about the impact commercial farming has on the environment and the cruelty that is often inherent to commercial farming.

> She would select her target audience to be people who are on the verge of making the transition, rather than disrupting a crowd so badly that they choke on their last bite of a chop or steak.

> She would refrain from actions causing damage to the properties of private people and entities and from disrupting their operations in such a manner that it damages their brand identity.

Can you see that in both cases the outcome is far more positive for all involved when the concern is approached with a wise mind?

Having a wise mind is not a genetic privilege nor based on class, gender, religion, or cultural distinction. It is an approach towards life, events, and others that we can all adapt to, learn and acquire.

DBT presented me with the steps I had to take to adapt my thinking and approach toward life from being ruled by my emotional mind to operating from a wise-mind perspective.

ESTABLISH CHANGE THROUGH RAIN

In DBT there are indeed many acronyms, each as meaningful as the next, and all of them are potent drivers of change to establish a meaningful life. RAIN is no different.

RAIN stands for recognize, accept, investigate, and not-identify. By following the steps captured in RAIN, you'll be able to successfully maintain an entirely different approach toward how you manage your emotions. RAIN is a way to practice mindfulness when your circumstances make it challenging to slip into a state of awareness.

The two most common unbalanced ways people approach emotions are either to allow them to run wild without applying any control over what is taking place, or to suppress the feeling so deeply that they lose circulation and become numb. Neither way resolves these feelings and the lack of addressing these feelings in an appropriate manner can resolve even greater concerns that will demand your attention.

Walk with me through the four steps of the process:

Recognize: It requires that you take a moment to recognize and identify the emotion that is welling up inside when you are becoming more emotionally charged. Instead of denying the presence of the emotion, acknowledge it without any judgment or self-criticism. Embrace the emotion by taking time to become aware of the physical sensation it leaves in your body. Instead of running away or suppressing, or even losing yourself in the emotion, just observe it and the impact it has.

✓ I love visualization and mostly find myself thinking in pictures. Yes, when I hear the word "cat," the image of a black cat immediately comes to mind. I've always found that images make it easier to explain and grasp certain concepts. So, I want to use an image here, too, to explain RAIN in a simpler manner.

✓ Now, back to the first step of RAIN: Visualize yourself standing on the edge of a lake. You can see the water, the trees seaming the edge of the lake, and maybe there are snowcapped mountains in the background. It can also be an ominous lake with a thick fog hanging low above the dark and murky water. You have the freedom to decide what your lake looks like, just remember that the lake in this image represents a specific emotion.

✓ As we know that you are observing the lake by looking at the details around it, it is certain that you aren't running away from the feeling nor suppressing it; but, you are also not going into the lake and immersing yourself in the water. No, you are standing on the edge, observing. You can name the lake—let's call this "lake rejection." So, appearance wise, this is probably leaning more toward the ominous and desolate side of options.

✓ By taking this step, you are creating distance between yourself and the emotion, making it easier to observe it and accept its existence.

Allow: As you accept the existence of the lake—or feeling—you let it be. You might not like the lake and it will surely not end on your list of preferred go-to holiday destinations, but you allow it to be present in your visualization. As you do this, your inherent resistance toward the lake's existence disappears gradually.

✓ So, you acknowledged and accepted the feeling you have—rejection in this example—without getting caught in it, allowing it to drag you down to a place of deep internal emotional torment.

Investigate: Fear is often rooted in the unknown. Therefore, it is something you can overcome by becoming more familiar with the things that scare you.

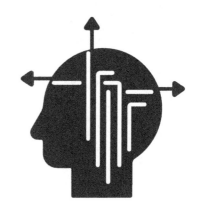

✓ At times, the scary things in life are dark & ominous, and at other times, it can be the hurt caused by rejection. However, we can explore the lake and notice that the water is in fact not dark and scary; it was merely a cloud in front of the sun casting a dark shadow on the surface. Similarly, you can notice that you were not rejected and that the friend who declined an invite is actually dealing with a very personal matter over which they are highly embarrassed and didn't want to share.

✓ You can also ask questions like why do you perceive the lake in this manner? Would it look different if you take 10 steps to the left or the right from where you are standing now? It mostly likely does. What do you need right now to take care of yourself in your situation?

✓ By asking these questions, you alert your conscious thinking to find solutions on how to best approach the manner to resolve the emotion you've identified.

Nonidentification: At the heart of this step is the realization that you are merely an observer of the lake, a visitor to that space in your mind. You aren't the lake itself. See, when I state that, you are probably thinking, Of course, I am not the lake. However, when we replace the term lake with a certain emotion, like rejection, it is so easy to consider ourselves to be rejected rather than merely experiencing the emotion—rejection.

✓ Remember, as much as you are not the lake, you are also not any other negative emotion threatening to take control of your mind, words, and actions. This may be the last step in the process, but it is crucial to maintain the distance, to acknowledge what you are experiencing but also understand that it is only a feeling or an experience. It is not who you are.

USING MEDITATION TO PROCESS EMOTIONS

I admit that when you are experiencing intense emotions, it may not be the best time or place for meditation. Yet, when you commit to regular meditation with the intent to improve your emotional management and have made the practice part of your daily routine, you are gradually equipping yourself with the tools needed, so that when that intense moment presents itself, you are prepared.

Through meditation, you can adjust your natural response to strong emotions, calm yourself, and process emotions that may still be suppressed and need to be aired before you can address them effectively.

There are several different forms of meditation and you can choose any way you like to meditate, or try a couple of methods and pick one that suits your personality and unique style best. Yet, at the foundation of many different meditative practices are the following steps:

1. Find a place where you can sit undisturbed.

2. Settle in a comfortable position, either lying down on your back or sitting in a position in which you are comfortable.

3. Decide how long you want to meditate and set a timer so that you don't have to watch the clock.

4. You can even wear comfortable clothes that won't distract you.

5. Many struggle initially to meditate effectively, but the more you do it, the better you become. As it can be hard to sit still for so long, start by setting your time for only five minutes—you can increase this later on.

6. Decide how long you want to meditate and set a timer so that you don't have to watch the clock.

Remember that the purpose of meditation isn't to clear your mind and think about nothing at all but to maintain your focus on one thing only. Every time that something else pops into your mind, you just gently nudge it away and return to what you've decided to focus on in the first place.

This "thing" you focus on can be a dot on the wall in front of you, an image you visualize, the tones of music—if you prefer to have music playing like the sounds of chimes or Buddhist bowls—your breathing, or even visualizing how anger leaves your body with every exhale and how clear and pure peace enters every time you inhale.

Gradually, you'll feel how relaxed your body is, but an even more significant event occurs on a mental level. You'll find that the more you meditate, the more you peel through the different layers of your anger, your emotions, and your being. You gain a deeper inherent clarity, calmness, and insight in matters that you've always struggled with. Through this connection, taking time out to commit yourself to self-development and growth, it is as if all forces come together to assist you on this noble quest.
I want to share with you what happened to me when I started meditating for the first time.

I had a quiet spot and found an app that would play lovely, soothing sounds. I would set my timer for 15 minutes and just lie down and breathe in and out until I could feel my muscles relaxing. Then, I would listen to the sounds, and whenever everyday life entered my thoughts, I would push them away.

Initially, when the image popped into my mind it made little sense to me. However, the same image kept on returning day after day. It was the image of a rusty old metal pole that towered high above my head, but it was more than that, as every day I would see how bits of rust would flake off the pole and gradually become less rusty. After a couple of days, I realized that these rusty bits were memories linked to my heavy burden of emotional baggage. Each time, the pole looked better than the previous time. After about two weeks, I could see the pole had a shiny surface.

I remember that by the time the pole turned into a bright and brilliant surface, I felt much lighter too. I was calmer and could approach explosive situations with reason and thought that allowed me to respond instead of react.

Nature gives preference to balance. It is continuously working towards sustaining an equilibrium, and the moment you open yourself to still the turbulent emotions inside, it gradually happens all by itself to you too. To me, that is how meditation became really beneficial on my journey to overcome my anger with the guidance of DBT.

What your meditation journey would look like is not going to be the same as mine. Your imagery will be completely unique to you, and how you benefit from the ancient practice will be answering your custom needs. But, you need to start to reap the benefits that can free you from the weight lying on your shoulders without proper emotional management. Claim your image, your healing, and the sense of progress as you work your way through the many layers of complexities making up your being.

DIGGING DEEPER

I am so tempted to make this assignment centered around meditation, as I know it will benefit you so much, but I don't, because I want these exercises to lead you to practical solutions you can apply in the heat of the moment. So, please start meditating today as you'll be doing yourself an immense favor.

Meanwhile, I also want you to grab your DBT journal and remember an incident where you reacted with an emotional response:

Instead of reliving the entire event in your mind, visualize the event from the top, but use RAIN to process what happened.

Accept that these emotions exist and that it is normal to feel them from time to time.

Recognize the emotions you've been feeling.

Nonidentify with these feelings by acknowledging that they are in you but not who you are.

Investigate these emotions.

Great!
Next, we are going to explore more fun ways to keep your cool and to allow your wise mind to flourish.

CHAPTER 6: KEEPING YOUR COOL

66

Emotions flow in and out, they don't define us.

99

– Julie Reed

One of the hardest realities of life to learn—whether you are 13, 30, or 83—life will always have hard times and good times, throw challenges at you, and place obstacles in your way. The worst of it all is that these things interrupt your rhythm usually when you least expect it.

Tracy's life was fine. She got good grades at school, just got chosen for the cheerleaders, and was looking forward to starting the final year of high school with a bang. One day as she walked in from school, she found her mother in tears on the couch with her dad sitting on the other side of the room looking very concerned and his hands folded in his lap. He was leaving them for another woman. Yes, Tracy knew that he didn't leave her, he was leaving his marriage with her mother, but it still felt like he was walking out on both of them, choosing someone else above her. What made it even worse for her was when she learned that her dad's mistress is the mother of one of the kids in her school—that sucked. Tracy told me that it felt like she was falling without stopping into a deep dark pit.

Darren's football career was going great. He knew he would be on the field to play the coming weekend when several college scouts would be in the crowd. His sister begged him to go horse riding with her that Wednesday, and while he has been very comfortable on a horse his entire life, his horse got spooked by a bee and the mare threw him off. Darren broke his leg in two places and was out for the season. Darren never returned to football at all again.

It can even be something as simple as oversleeping; getting dressed when you are already late and a zipper breaks; or not being able to find your favorite scarf, shoes, or clean underwear. These things happen. We can't stop them. They happen to you and to me, and all we can do about it is to learn the skills to maintain our balance and not allow them to throw us off track.

There is a saying that if you have $86,400 in your bank account—that is how many seconds you have in a day—and someone steals $10 of it, you are not going to throw the remaining $83,390 away. Why do we do it with our time then? Money can be replaced; time can't.

HOW TO KEEP YOUR EMOTIONS IN CHECK

Emotional balance refers to your ability to balance the positive and negative feelings you have and to sustain this balance regardless of what is happening around you. The image I get when I think about emotional balance is that of a surfer riding the waves with ease regardless of what the water is doing underneath the board.

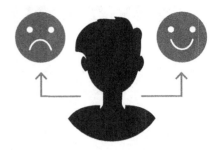

I guess the same is true for a skier, skateboarder, or when you are on a hoverboard; these people are all highly skilled to sustain their balance with mostly nothing but a few core movements. They make it look so easy, but they are only so successful because they practiced it a lot.

You can do the same and achieve the same effortless appearance when you are sustaining your emotional balance, but it will require practicing the correct skills.

SET THE STAGE

What I mean when I say you need to "set the stage" is that you have to take preventative measures to avoid being caught in the perfect storm. This would mean that you get enough sleep—a tired mind is much easier to get overwhelmed by negative emotions. By practicing mindfulness, you'll be more aware of the feelings you have and be able to identify them as well as address the root of these concerns. When you notice that your emotional state is manifesting physically—you may have a constant headache, regular stomach cramps, or just feel physically drained or highly strung—act on these symptoms and address them immediately. Take a time out, go for a walk in nature, or have a coffee with a friend. Whatever it is you do, give your mind and body a timeout to relax and recover. Taking regular breaks prevents major emotional explosions or even implosions, causing you to collapse internally.

Another way that can help you to set a stage that is far more resilient is to stay connected with those you love and who care about you too. These people are your support network and can hold you up when you are feeling weak. Take care of yourself and be kind to yourself. Take that long bath when you feel you need it, or have that night out with friends to get a break from all the stress you experience at school.

Never underestimate the importance of gratitude. Make being grateful a part of your daily routine and see how much easier the challenge along your journey becomes to handle confidently. Emotional balance is also easier to sustain when you have physical balance too; yes, work hard, but also take breaks to be active. The fitter your body is, the more capable you'll be to address emotional and mental challenges with ease.

When you are active, trying to do so outside for nature is still the most effective environment to calm down turbulent emotions.

By setting the stage with these actions, you know you have a strong foundation to overcome obstacles with confidence and without allowing their emotional charge to overpower you.

Setting the stage is the most important step you can take to ensure effective emotional regulation, but it isn't all you can do.

TAKE STOCK OF THE IMPACT OF THESE EMOTIONS

While setting the stage will help you overcome these challenges, it won't indemnify you from being hit by these storms. So, when you are hit by a storm, assess the impact of the emotions you are feeling:

Are you so upset by your friend being constantly late for appointments that you'll allow your anger to ruin a life-long friendship?

Are you so hurt by the actions of a loved one that you want to amputate them from your life forever?

Are you feeling so despondent about not making the team that you aren't even willing to support them next to the field, or try out ever again?

Whatever emotion you are feeling fueling your anger, determine the amount of damage caused in your life or relationships and compare this to the value you attach to whatever is at risk to decide whether you can let go of these emotions or are willing to rather risk losing it all. In a sense, it is not only a damage assessment but also a risk forecast.

MANAGE INSTEAD OF REPRESS

The speed and grace of the surfer won't be possible if they tried to repress the impact of the waves on the board. Quite frankly, I think any other approach than merely managing the state of the water and the waves will crush the surfer, as the force they are up against is simply so overpowering. The same is true for emotions: For a while, it may appear as if you are doing great by repressing your feelings, but in the end, their force will overwhelm you. The solution would be to apply all the techniques you've learned so far, like breathing deeply or writing in your journal, to manage what you are feeling.

USING
OPPOSITE-TO-EMOTION ACTION

This is another very helpful exercise DBT taught me, and I am sure you'll gain a lot of value from it too. The best thing is that you may already be doing this in your life, so the exercise will only help you to get better at it and guide you towards how many other situations you can use it.

It is something I do almost on a daily basis, and I can specifically recall a moment when I applied it earlier today.

I was working late last night, got to bed way past my usual bedtime, and overslept this morning. I admit that I wasn't setting the right stage for emotional balance and I nearly paid the price for my negligence in this regard. I was heading out, and my neighbor knocked on my door. She is a very old lady with a high demand to make small talk. She wanted to borrow some sugar and immediately plunged into giving me the latest updates on all 23 of her grandkids. I didn't have time to listen to her and desperately wanted to snub the conversation with a rude comment, but I applied the opposite emotion, and said, "Debra, what about I pop in later this afternoon and then you tell me all about it over a cup of coffee?"

It worked. I managed to arrive on time at my appointment and didn't hurt anyone's feelings or get any haters in the process.

The exercise requires that you identify what you are feeling at that very moment. Then, consider how you want to react. Next... you do the opposite.

I was frustrated and annoyed by my neighbor. I wanted to tell her that I don't have time for all her stories and that she talks way too much, but I politely scheduled another time to give her all my attention.

The mean girl at school asks you if you bought your dress at Goodwill. You are hurt and angered by her comment as you think you have a great personal style. You want to grab her by her hair and pull her through the mud. But you stop, look at her, and politely say, "No, but thanks for noticing anyway," as you walk away from the explosive situation.

Or, maybe you were not chosen for your team at school. You are angry at the coach and feel that nobody on the team deserves it as much as you do. You never want to play again, but you continue to go to the practices and improve your game while supporting them next to the field when they play.

ESTABLISH CHANGE THROUGH RAIN

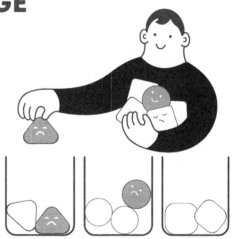

The more you are mindful, the better your awareness of your emotions becomes and the better you'll get at managing them. It is just like driving a car. Maybe you've got your driver's permit already, or maybe you are still working towards achieving that milestone. Either way, when you first got in behind a steering wheel, it was most likely a daunting experience. You are in charge of a powerful machine that can hurt or even kill others—or yourself.

There are pedals, levers, and a stick you have to control. Then, you have to find the balance between pressing the fuel pedal hard enough to move forward but not too hard so that you speed. It is daunting, and I haven't even gotten yet to discussing the road rules and signs, lanes, pedestrians, and other vehicles sharing the same road. Yet, after spending a bit of time driving, you get familiar with the vehicle and how to negotiate it through heavy traffic.

The first time I got safely to my destination, I felt a sense of accomplishment for doing it and relief that I didn't hit anyone nor damaged the car. Now, it is easy.

The same is true when it comes to your emotions. The more you are aware of them, dissect and explore them, the easier it becomes to manage them effectively even while moving through a minefield of possible emotional outbursts. Yet, it is not the only benefit you'll reap when you start to explore your emotions. No, you'll also prevent yourself from feeling the burden of meta-emotions.

What are meta-emotions? Meta-emotions are the feelings you feel caused by other feelings you are feeling. I know, that is a tongue-twister, but it sounds more complex than it is.

Sarah and Claud have been dating for three months. Sarah is smitten. Claude is her first love and she is just so happy to be in a relationship. After school, she gets home and falls onto her bed to check her phone. She immediately notices a notification that Claude sent her a text.

CLAUDE

Hi, S. I've been thinking and I think we need to give each other space and see other people. Cool. CU. PS. I'm taking Amy to the dance.

What? Sarah is immediately in tears while the following questions run through her mind:

What did I do wrong?

Why did he leave me?

We were still good only a few hours ago, what happened?

Nobody will like me ever again.

I am such a loser.

Am I not pretty enough?

Is it because I didn't sleep with him yet?

I should've said yes when we spoke about sex, but I wasn't ready.

Did he just break off with me over a text?

Who does he think he is?

Who is Amy?

Argh, why did I cry?

No wonder he left you, Sarah. You cry over nothing.

Why do I always cry? I hate it when I cry. I am so ticked off at myself right now!

Initially, Sarah felt hurt, heartache, and rejection. These are all reasonable emotions and it is normal for her to feel that way. But as time passed, she developed a meta-emotion: anger. Now, she is angry at herself for being sad over her loser ex-boyfriend who didn't even have the guts to break it off with her in person.

Sarah's initial emotions were validated. The meta-emotion, anger, is only an added burden, something to leave her feeling ashamed.

When you are mindful of what you are feeling, and understand why you are feeling a certain way and that it is okay to feel that way, you stop meta-emotions from developing.

What Sarah could've done was explore what she was feeling. Then, she could have determined that she felt shocked as it came out of the blue. She would've noticed that she was feeling heartache, for she truly liked Claude a lot. She might even have felt that he betrayed her every time he told her how much he likes her, for clearly, he was lying. If anger did show up, then it would've been anger towards Claude for fooling her to think that his feelings were sincere, for breaking it off with her in a text message, and for not keeping his word by going to the dance with her. While there are several reasons to be angry at him, getting angry with herself for displaying perfectly normal feelings would do her no good.

ACCEPTING THE PAIN AND MOVING ON

I can hear you say, "So, what must Sarah do, for not being angry at herself is not helping much now, is it?"

Well, the reality of life—heads up, this can be a hard one to swallow—is that we can't control everything that happens to us and we are bound to get hurt at times. We can try our best to prevent this from happening, but there are no certainties that it won't happen from time to time. So, yes, Claude hurt Sarah. But, we often increase the intensity of the hurt when we decide to hold onto it.

Sometimes, we need to acknowledge the things or people that are already gone from our lives rather than desperately try to hold onto the idea of changing the situation. Similarly, the only usual remedy in life is to accept that you've been caused to experience pain and that you have to move on, for staying will only make the hurt worse and last far longer.

DBT offers you three skills to help you through this challenging time and ease the suffering you experience. These three skills are all part of the process of accepting reality, supporting you to manage your emotions more effectively even when in tough times.

While it may feel like you would be better off rejecting or ignoring your feelings, both options are toxic coping mechanisms. The following three methods are far more emotionally healthy alternatives.

RADICAL ACCEPTANCE

When you take a moment to put your feelings aside, what does reality look like? It is important to understand the details of the reality of your situation because that is what you need to accept. The longer you are going to fight, resist, or reject reality, the more you are only wearing yourself down emotionally, mentally, and physically. The moment you stop to interact with the pain, shame, rejection, disappointment, or any other negative emotion, it becomes better and the healing can begin.

It can be a hard thing to do, but it is very much the same as scratching off the scab from a wound. Every time you scratch the injury, it starts to bleed again. However, by doing so, you are also increasing the risk of infection and causing the wound to leave an even more pronounced scar than if you only left it to heal.

When you apply radical acceptance, you can distinguish between the things you can control—like your choices, outcomes, words, and behavior—and you stop wasting your energy on the things you can't control—the choices, outcomes, words, and behavior of others.

I want you to always remember that you are supposed to feel your emotions, acknowledge them, embrace them, accept them, learn from them, and heal from them. Never are you ever asked to become a slave to your emotions. The choice remains yours.

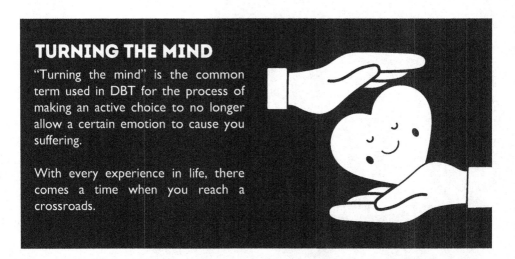

TURNING THE MIND

"Turning the mind" is the common term used in DBT for the process of making an active choice to no longer allow a certain emotion to cause you suffering.

With every experience in life, there comes a time when you reach a crossroads.

On the one hand, you have the choice to remain controlled by the emotion and to allow the pain to continue. Gradually, the pain has developed meta-emotions, and you now have an even heavier burden to carry with you. When you look down the other pathway, you see acceptance leading gradually into growth and healing. Down this pathway, your pain decreases over time, and you become wiser, stronger, and better equipped to deal with the challenges life will continue to throw at you—not because of your nature, but because of the nature of life.

TURNING THE MIND

Willingness is often underestimated as a part of the healing process, or any growth for that matter. I can share the most significant and powerful steps to help you to achieve the results you desire. Yet, they are all utterly meaningless if they aren't met with willingness. To overcome the pain you are feeling, accept the feelings you have, learn from your emotions, and become skilled at managing your emotions in a manner that you can enjoy a balanced life demands your willingness to let go, learn, accept, apply, and enrich your life. It demands no less of a willingness than what it demanded of the surfer gliding smoothly and effortlessly at top speeds, mastering the powerful waves of the ocean.

Like how salt adds flavor to food, willingness brings success to your efforts to establish change.

Are you willing to do what it takes to master the waves of emotions caused by the unexpected twists and rocks on the journey of life?

DIGGING DEEPER

Time to grab your DBT journal again. This time, I want you to pick a situation in your life that you are struggling to accept and let go of the emotions it causes you to feel. I find the following exercise very helpful (Skyland Trail, 2019):

1. What are you fighting against, or what is the reality of the situation? For Sarah, the reality is that maybe Claude just didn't feel the same way. It is also that someone who breaks off a relationship via a text is really not the kind of person you want to be with.

2. Remind yourself that the reality of the situation can't be changed. For Sarah, the reality is also that she really liked him and he was her first love, yet he hurt her badly and there is nothing she can do about it now.

3. As it is usually the case that something led to the situation you find yourself in, determine what that "thing" was that caused it all. Maybe Claude always liked Amy, but because she wasn't interested, he went for Sarah instead, and only then did Amy become interested. I know it is horrible, but this is just an example.

4. Take a few deep breaths to calm your thoughts and relax your body.

5. Compile a list of the things you feel like doing if you choose not to accept reality.

6. Determine why these are all bad moves to make. You might have to think about what may happen in the future if you take these steps too.

7. Become aware of the feelings you have and the sensations they cause in your body.

8. Consider how much you have to live for if you remove the pain from the equation for a moment. Sarah still had a lot of friends, a loving family, good marks, a great social circle, and did well in sports.

9. Become aware of how focusing on the positives in your life make you feel.

10. Decide to instead focus on these good things in your life and enjoy the feelings they create.

Every time you fall back into a state of misery, remind yourself that you did put a lot of thought into the process and that you've made a choice about what you are doing. Then, gently nudge your thoughts back to what is good in your life.

CHAPTER 7: USING YOUR WORDS

> **Words have the power to both destroy & heal.**
>
> *—Buddha*

It was playwright Edward Bulwer-Lytton who advised the world about the power of words when he said that the pen is mightier than the sword. Strangely enough, we tend to fear war, nuclear attacks, or any other form of physical harm, while often the power of our words is widely underestimated. Your words can hurt or heal, but they also have the power to bring about change, repair, restore, build, encourage, transform, or be effective in any other way you choose. How good you'll be at achieving the outcome you've set out for will depend on how skilled you are at using your words.

The degree to which you are effective in communication will largely determine the quality of your relationships, how successful you are in achieving your dreams and even impact your overall happiness. DBT taught me the communication skills needed to have healthy relationships, and I am passing this wisdom on to you. The four skills I consider to be vital to my overall happiness are called THINK, FAST, GIVE, and DEAR MAN.

THINK

THINK is one of the more recently added skills to DBT and is an acronym for think, have empathy, interpretations, notice, and kindness. The main aim of THINK is to minimize the bad emotions you feel toward others. It is hard enough to be in control of your words when you are not in a good space, and when you are feeling negativity toward another person—may they be a family member, friend, romantic partner, or even a stranger—it can be almost impossible to manage what you say effectively. Therefore, this strategy is so helpful. It simply eases all the negativity in your mind around someone and makes effective communication so much easier:

THINK:

This part of the process asks that you put yourself in the other person's shoes. Consider how they feel or think. What are they thinking about you?

Do they see you as a threat? Maybe they are hurt by something you aren't even aware of.

A while ago, I was waiting in line at the DMV when I overheard a conversation taking place behind me. It was two ladies, both moms of teenage boys who were sharing their sorrows with each other. They were mentioning how angry their kids are and how concerned they are about the future, as neither knew why their children were so angry nor what to do about it. I remembered how my path randomly crossed with DBT, and I decided to turn around and share a bit about my story and how DBT can help. They were very interested but asked that I spoke to their kids, and I agreed. The topic of communication came up while I chatted with one kid, who got visibly upset when I shared this strategy, about how he needs to think about the other person's perspective. He felt it is unfair that I could suggest that he has to go to all the effort of changing his perspective. He was a football player and loved the game, so I explained THINK in the following manner: Imagine you are playing the game of a lifetime. Whether your team will go to compete on the state level depends on winning this game and the stakes are high. But, your team remains a bit behind the entire time as you can't read the opposition's next move. Time after time, they catch you off guard. You know you'll lose. Then, during a break, you get the opportunity to see how the other team sees you. You get to think like they think and where they see your weak spots. This knowledge gives you the edge to pick up your game, win, and go to the state championship. Will you consider this as an effort or as a golden opportunity to achieve the outcome you desire? Obviously the latter, right? The same happens when you put yourself in the shoes of someone else. You get to understand what they are feeling and can address the matter more effectively from your side. By changing your perspective, you give yourself the edge in a conversation.

HAVE EMPATHY:

When you understand the other person's side, it becomes easier to feel what they feel. When you have a greater understanding of their side of the story, it is easier to feel empathy for them and to tone down the intensity of your emotions.

INTERPRETATION:

Stepping into the other person's shoes will also help you to grasp a greater understanding of why they are doing what they do. It gives you a much deeper insight into the situation, which is often all we need to gain a better understanding and resolve the matter without causing any more hurt to another or ourselves.

NOTICE:

When you look at the other person, what do you see? It is hard to see someone else for who they truly are if your vision is tainted with a negative perspective and when you can't see beyond your own emotions. Therefore, shake your assumptions and look at the person for who they really are.

KINDNESS:

Keep all of the above in mind when you respond, and then do so with kindness. Kindness doesn't mean that you are breaking yourself to accommodate the other or that you disregard your emotions to spare theirs. No, it means that you are setting your boundaries but are doing so with kindness. Rather than saying, "I can't stand to be near you and I don't want to see you ever again," respond with, "I am hurt and angry and I can't resolve this matter now. Give me some time to cool down and, when I am ready, I'll reach & and we can talk then." It is really as simple as that.

FAST

Fair, (no) apologies, stick to your values, and truthful is the framework of FAST. FAST is all about setting your boundaries and protecting them to secure your self-respect when conflict arises:

FAIR:

Fairness towards yourself and others is woven into the fibers of having self-respect. Someone who portrays self-respect is fair in their behavior, words, and even thoughts. They will treat others in the same manner as they want to be treated and, by doing so, they steer clear from being dramatical or judgy in their approach towards others. They don't distinguish people based on any presumptions and always ask themselves what is the right thing to do, for them and you.

(NO) APOLOGIES:

Yes, there will be times—and probably many times too—when you have to apologize. You just don't ever have to apologize for something you didn't do.

STICK TO YOUR VALUES:

If you aren't going to stand for anything, you'll likely fall for everything. So, define your values and stick to them.

Don't associate yourself with people who contest your values the entire time—nobody needs that added stress in their lives. Rather, spend your time with people who are like-minded and supportive. It is also important that you are true to your values. If you state that education is important to you, then make the most of your education and don't be a slacker at school. If you value change and state that you want to see an improvement in the world, then be the change you want to see. There is no better way to celebrate what you stand for and what your values are than actually living according to them.

TRUTHFUL:

Be honest to yourself and others but also about yourself and others. Being truthful will sometimes be hard. It means that you can't exaggerate, be dramatic, or oversimplify your situation. At times, being truthful can leave you feeling embarrassed or ashamed. Yet, if you want to live your life with dignity, confidence, joy, and have healthy relationships, it will demand some investment from your side. Neglecting the four steps of FAST is the fastest way to ruin your relationships and your reputation.

GIVE

GIVE—the key to healthy and happy relationships, regardless of who the other person is—stands for gentle, interested, validate, and easy manner.

While GIVE will help you to sustain your relationships, it is also beneficial when you meet new people:

GENTLE:

Take a moment to consider your general approach towards people. Would you describe it as forceful, making a statement, being on defense—even attacking—or are you gentle? The way we approach and address others often determines the way they'll respond. If you are going in with force, then they may offer instant resistance. Similarly, if you open with an attack, the immediate response is to become defensive and close up toward the person launching this attack. However, choose to approach them gently and people are generally more open to sharing, collaborating, or discussing the matter you want to address. Similarly, the way you approach someone whom you meet for the very first time, determines the first impression you leave with them. You'll get much further in life and enjoy far greater success with a gentle approach toward people.

INTEREST:

Have you ever experienced that deeply satisfying feeling when you've spoken to someone and they just made you feel heard? The entire time you were talking, you could see they were listening to every word you said. Their body language and expressions communicated that they absorbed your message, and they followed through on the conversation by asking you questions to learn more and gain a deeper understanding. You, too, can be that person when you show genuine interest in the other person.

VALIDATE:

Validation means that you verbally express that you understand what the other person is saying. You'll use statements that echo the feelings they are expressing. Do not undervalue validation in a conversation. Just imagine a situation where you are telling your best friend, "I am so angry right now. It is the third time now that my lab assistant left me to clean up our station on my own. It is not fair. We both worked on the project but when the period is over, she leaves me with all the dirty equipment."

 Which of the following replies would mean the most to you?

> "Aha. Is that cute guy still in your class? He looks so hot in his lab coat."

> Or, "No way! That's not right. How unfair. I mean, can't the teacher see what she is doing? I would be so angry as well if I were you. Maybe you should tell her next time straight out that it is her turn to clean up."

 See the big difference validation can bring to any conversation? Use it to your benefit

EASY MANNER:

I have to share this story with you. I was about 15 when my school sent a couple of us to go camping with several students from the surrounding school to explore nature. It was a type of adventure camp and we lived in tents and had to study nature. It was fun, but then I had a tent mate, Eileen. She was worried about everything and so intense about every little detail. Whenever we had to do something together, she would get so stressed out and, eventually, turned me into a nervous wreck too. While we promised to keep in contact after, I blocked her number on my phone the moment our bus departed.

A much better approach towards others would be to present yourself as easygoing. When you are easygoing, you still take life seriously and know what is important, but you are also confident enough in your skills and abilities that the challenges ahead don't freak you out. Your approach will also likely calm others down, making life a lot easier for everyone.

DEAR MAN

Sometimes, you need effective communication skills to say something or to make a statement, and at times, you need these skills to ask for something in a manner that will support your effort to get what you are looking for. It is in these situations when DEAR MAN can be especially helpful.

DEAR MAN is another DBT acronym for describe, express, assert, reinforce, mindful, appear confident, and negotiate:

DESCRIBE:

Okay, I think this is relatively straightforward. When you want something from someone, you need to describe to them what you want, or how else would they know what it is that you are asking? When you want to go to the movies with friends but would need your parents' permission to go—and some pocket money too—the best approach is to describe what you want from them. Do so politely but be clear about it. Look at the following three examples and see if you can see which would be the most effective to get the results you desire in this case.

✓ "Emma, Jason, everyone is going to watch a movie tonight. It sounds like so much fun. I wish I could go too."

✓ "I think it is time that you spoil me, as I've been slaving away the past couple of months. My friends are all going to the movies tonight and I deserve to go too."

✓ "My friends are all going to the movies tonight and I would really want to go too. Would it be okay if I go? I would need about $30 though, but don't worry, Emma and Jason will fetch me and drop me off, so I'll be home by 11."

» The first two attempts were not really describing the details of the event or even asked for anything for that matter. The first is more a hint and the second a demand. The third option clearly and politely states what is desired.

EXPRESS:

Part of the success of the third option is that it expresses exactly what you desire. You stated what you want to do, how much money you would need, and what the logistics around the situation would be like.

ASSERT:

You can say why something is important to you and be assertive without being arrogant, demanding, or aggressive. Most people respond better when you clarify why you think you deserve that they grant your request without coming across as if you think they'll be utterly wrong if they don't. Assertiveness is often coming across more in your body language and the tone you use than in your words. So, keep eye contact and stand up straight.

REINFORCE:

You should use reinforcement as the sequel to your request. First, you asked for something, and when your request is granted or it seems like matters are going in a positive direction for you, you can reinforce why granting your request is good. Examples will be, "I'll be back by 11," or "I promise I'll mow the lawn," "do the laundry," or "the dishes." Then, of course, stick to the promises you make.

MINDFUL:

Whether you are identifying your emotions, enjoying a meal, or asking for what you want, remain in the moment and be mindful. In this example, it will be beneficial to remain mindful, as you'll be able to better observe your parent's response, facial expression, or any nonverbal sounds. You'll also be able to think on your feet and know when you need to start negotiating so that you don't miss out on the opportunity.

APPEAR CONFIDENT:

Would you be more inclined to give someone what they ask of you when they come across confident and are presenting their request with clarity and the conviction that you'll see the matter in the same way as they do, or when they barely get their words out?

If you've given your request thought and followed every step of the DEAR MAN approach, then there is no reason why you can't be confident. For example, is there any reason why your request to the movies may be declined? Did you pick a good time to ask for this? Have you taken all possible factors into consideration of why it may not happen? If so, then you've covered all that you had to do.

NEGOTIATE:

Negotiation is only necessary when it appears like you are not going to get what you want. Don't start negotiating before that moment appears, but it will help to prepare yourself beforehand for if the moment occurs. Make sure you have a valid argument and good reasons for why you think your request should be granted. What would such a negotiation look like? Maybe offer to do something in return, to earn the money you are asking for, or commit to not asking anything for the rest of the month.

Always make sure that you know the person you are asking this favor from and understand what is important to them; you'll know how to speak to their hearts and minds more effectively.

If you approach communication like an art, realizing the power of your words, the tone you use, your body language, and your facial expressions, you'll be much more effective in sustaining healthy and lasting relationships. The added benefit is of course also that you'll be able to avoid a lot of anger or negative energy from your life, making it much easier to manage your emotions.

DIGGING DEEPER

Each of these communication skill sets is aimed to address a specific kind of communication and will be of value to address a specific need you may have:

THINK is ideally used in conflict situations and to resolve the matter before it spins out of control.

FAST will help you to express yourself with confidence & help to establish boundaries to protect your values.

GIVE will support your efforts to grow your existing bonds stronger and to make new friends.

The steps of DEAR MAN will help you to get what you ask for in life.

Each of these will help you get through your teenage years with much greater success and living with—but also causing far fewer—emotional scars. Yet, once you've mastered each of these techniques, they'll become the various foundations of communication you'll need to be successful in your career and adult relationships too.

Therefore, I want you to practice each of these skills from now onwards and not favor one above another. To help you to get comfortable with at least one straight away, I want you to think about what is that one challenging conversation that is coming up soon. It can be a difficult conversation you need to have with a friend with whom you had an argument and still need to make things right. Then, you'll need to use THINK. Perhaps a friend is disregarding your values and you have to assert yourself with FAST. You can also feel uneasy about going to a new school soon, and the fact that you have to make new friends. GIVE will be helpful, and if you want to ask a favor from a parent, friend, or teacher, then use DEAR MAN.

You pick the situation relevant to your life right now and plan in your DBT journal how you'll approach the conversation based on the different steps of the relevant DBT communication skill.

Capture the options you have under every step and visualize how this conversation is going to work out. Once you've had the conversation, return to your journal and record what you think went really well as well as what you can do to improve your approach.

CHAPTER 8:
PUTTING IT ALL TOGETHER

> 66 The great thing in this world is not so much where you stand as what direction you are moving. 99
>
> —Oliver Wendell Holmes

You have no control over all that has happened in your past. You can't undo the things you did, nor can you unsay the things you've said during those moments of erupted anger when you've lost all control. There is no point in pondering on these moments covered in shame, humiliation, embarrassment, or guilt. What you can do, though, is to take control over your words and actions, manage your emotions, and improve the image you have of your future.

Even the slightest change you make today has the possibility to ripple out and have a gigantic impact on your life lying ahead. One day, an excited woman met a complete stranger in a miserable state at a coffee vendor, and by taking the time to share all she knew about DBT, she changed the life of that woman and all who love her. I know that woman is me. If it wasn't for the stranger getting a coffee, I wouldn't have gotten to the point of writing this book for you to read. Can you see how far our actions ripple out, affecting people we don't even know?

HOW TO USE THE SHARED KNOWLEDGE AND SKILLS EFFECTIVELY

You have been introduced to some of the most effective and impactful DBT skills, but it may be confusing to determine where to go next. Sometimes, it helps to get a bird's eye view of the path you are not taking to assist you in clearly defining the road you are taking. I think giving you this bird's eye view on DBT will be the final skill I'll be adding to your toolbox.

Essentially, DBT consists of four modules each addressing an area of concern. The four stages are mindfulness, improving distress tolerance, getting better at managing your emotions, and improving your relationships through interpersonal effectiveness.

All four of these modules or stages flow from one to the other. For example, when you become more mindful, you'll get better at identifying your emotions, determining the actual cause of this stress, and managing your distress, consequently improving your relationships. It is why making changes by focusing on one area will improve the others too. But, if you want to enjoy more significant results, it is best to include daily changes in your life that will impact each of these areas individually. It is also why I've given you practical examples of each of these four stages.

As you know, my initial introduction to DBT was rather random, and a lot of what I've learned during the first couple of weeks was through self-study. As I wasn't exactly sure what I was doing, my approach to DBT was rather fast and loose. I lacked discipline, and most of it was rather unstructured or properly planned. I knew I didn't want to be so angry anymore and that my anger and the outbursts that went along with it were hurting the people I love as well as myself. However, when I found the structure I was looking for and could determine what I wanted to achieve by practicing the skill sets I've shared with you, I had direction and focus and my efforts became more effective.

Therefore, I want to recap on what it is you would want to achieve in each of the four DBT modules, to give you the direction which will assist you in making the progress you desire.

MINDFULNESS

Mindfulness improves your skills to observe your environment, both externally and internally. It helps to familiarize yourself with what you feel, ask what causes you to feel this way, and determine whether you are able to make any changes to better your situation or whether healing lies in acceptance. Then, it will also help you to remain mentally present in the moment, which will reduce your worries and anxiety over the future as well as your regrets over past events.

We can divide mindfulness skills into three stages. The one category includes ways to help you cope with your current situation. This is possible by improving the way you observe things, circumstances, and people without judgment. It is all about unbiased awareness. The second focuses on getting better at describing the things you observe. Effectively and accurately put into words what you experience can be challenging at times, but practice makes it far easier to achieve. The third leg is participating and would include yourself as an object to observe. Yes, you are not only getting more efficient in observing and describing external, but also internal, awareness.

The second category of mindfulness skills is coping skills. Firstly, they teach you to become less judgmental in your approach and the words you use. Secondly, it also includes being one-minded in the sense that you learn to focus on one thing at a time and avoid multitasking. Thirdly, it can enhance your effectiveness, your ability to learn how you can become more effective, and clarifies what practices help you the most to achieve a greater sense of mindfulness.

DISTRESS TOLERANCE

Life happens to all of us, regardless of our age or situation. In other words, during the times we get hurt, face stressful times, and are rejected and disappointed, we still need to keep our chin up high—crashing and burning is not an option. Through distress-tolerance skills, you'll get better at dealing with life when it becomes so hard. Grounding yourself is one of the very helpful techniques to master in this module.

EMOTIONAL REGULATION

The skills captured in this module aim to help you to master your emotions instead of succumbing your power to what you are feeling. It requires that you learn to assess every emotion to determine whether it is real or not, as well as whether it is a meta-emotion or a primary one. You also need to discern between which emotions you can change and which demand acceptance as they are relative to circumstances beyond your control. Once you've gotten a firm grasp on your emotions, it is vital that you learn to react to them in the most appropriate manner. Here, the opposite emotion skills are often the hardest to follow, but they also bring exceptional results.

IMPROVING YOUR RELATIONSHIPS

Nobody can make you happy—not your parents, siblings, romantic partners, or even your best friend. They can all contribute to your happiness, but you need to be happy within yourself to have lasting and happy relationships with them all. The more you improve your internal environment and become more content and in control of your life you are, the better these relationships will become too.

Furthermore, remember that when a volcano bursts open and spews molten rock into the air, it is not the volcano that gets hurt in the process. No, the volcano feels a welcome release of built-up pressure. It is, however, the vegetation and any houses in the area that get scorched, & it is the communities that get displaced by the hot lava covering everything they treasure.

The same happens when you are exploding. Immediately, you feel an immense release of anger and other suppressed emotions, but the pain and damage are caused to those who are close to you, your family, friends, and all those who love a volcano enough to put themselves in harm's way. So, by becoming a master of your emotions, being more mindful, and getting better at managing yourself during times of distress, you are also taking care of the relationships you have in your life. You are effectively deciding to become a dormant volcano, no longer threatening those around you.

Even though I am no expert in soil science, I am an avid gardener and have learned that volcano ash is an extremely rich fertilizer, and many plants flourish in nutrient-rich soil once the volcano has stopped erupting and turns dormant. None of the relationships you've destroyed or harmed through the many, many explosions during the years are unsalvageable. Once you become dormant in your anger, you can transform these relationships and help them to flourish just like the rich vegetation we'll find in volcano ash.

UNLEARNING OLD HABITS

The process of learning new skills and habits is a dual process, as you are effectively also unlearning old habits. For every skill that you are working on and getting better at, you are letting go of an existing habit that you've relied upon probably for quite some time.

Just like a caterpillar needs to shed old habits to move onto the next stage and become a butterfly, you, too, have to go through a transformation process to be able to fly. Nature is of course a huge aid in the caterpillar's quest for transformation and it is not so lenient to us mortals, but the following steps will be helpful to you:

ACKNOWLEDGE THAT YOU HAVE A PROBLEM.

Change is hard—very hard at times—and you need to have absolute clarity on why you want to make these changes in your life. Consider what your life would be like in a couple of years from now if you continue in the same manner, and compare that to what your life can be like if you make the necessary changes.

IDENTIFY THE HABITS THAT YOU KNOW YOU NEED TO SHED.

Determine why they are so toxic and what the consequences would be if they remain in your life any longer.

KNOW THAT THE JOURNEY TO SUCCESS COMES WITH MANY UPS AND DOWNS.

It is hardly ever the case that anyone sets out to bring significant change to their lives without regressing at some stage. Therefore, understand that change comes in a cycle.

First, you won't know that your behavior is a problem. Then, you become aware of how bad your anger outbursts are for you and those around you. Next, you are trying to devise a plan to change this situation, which is likely where you are now. The fourth stage comprises action. Now, you are knee-deep in learning new skills. However, as you gradually feel the conditions that initially drove you to change ease, it is easy to become slack. It is when you may skip your mindfulness exercises or meditation, or feel too tired to write in your DBT journal. So, the next stage is often regression, and then you start all over again; or, as you know about the blind spots in the cycle of change now, you can choose to continue your efforts and enjoy change.

START BY TAKING SMALL STEPS.

Small but consistent steps will get you much further than taking huge leaps which you can't sustain.

KNOW WHEN TO ASK FOR HELP.

We all need help at times, and now that you've learned the DEAR MAN skills, reach out & ask for help when you need it.

DIGGING DEEPER

Are you ready for your last guided exercise from me?

I want you to spend a bit of time on this exercise, so maybe find a spot where you can sit undisturbed and truly have the time to dig deep.

Now, list the habits you think you need to change. Then, for every habit, answer the following questions:

- ✓ What am I doing that is a problem?
- ✓ Why is it a problem?
- ✓ To whom is this a problem?
- ✓ What is going to happen if I don't change my behavior?
- ✓ What is going to happen if I don't change my behavior?
- ✓ What can my life look like if I do make the necessary changes?
- ✓ Does the value I attach to my current problematic behavior even measure up against what I can gain from making these changes?
- ✓ What obstacles can I expect along the way? In this question, consider the fact that you may lose some people whom you've considered to be friends.

A few years ago, I met Carl. Carl's anger was fueled by the people he surrounded himself with every day at school. They were a group of youngsters who would gather and energize themselves by watching the impact of their destructive behavior. They were responsible for several graffiti incidents at their school and the other students almost feared them as they were such an explosive bunch of kids hanging out together. Yet, Carl wanted to change and he had to prepare himself to lose these people. For a certain time, he became the person they zoomed their focus on, but in Carl's words, "Knowing what I know now, it was all worth it."

> Linked to the previous question is my last and final question: Who would you like to be friends with in the future you are preparing for yourself?

When you have absolute clarity on all these points, there is no more reason to hang onto your old life, simply because it is familiar. Then, you are heading in the right direction, you only need to take that very important first step.

CONCLUSION

> 66
> **The past cannot be changed. The future is yet in your power.**
> 99
> *-Mary Pickford*

One of the most frustrating things is to acknowledge you have a problem, to start working on it—like reading this book—by practicing the steps as you go along, and then... you don't see any immediate change.

This has been such a major challenge for me, and I can only imagine that it is even worse for you. When I was a teenager, life was just a little slower than it is now. The reality is that technology has transformed us into a generation of people used to instant gratification.

When I say instant gratification, I mean that if you want to know if a centipede really has 1,000 legs, you ask Google and yield multiple answers within seconds. When you see a pair of sneakers you like online, you press add to cart, complete the transaction, and within a couple of days, it arrives at your door. We don't have to wait long for anything really, except the processes that remain dependent on the human mind.

The mind hasn't evolved with technology. Sure, we are capable of working with all the advanced tools we have access to, but our minds didn't change much over the past couple of centuries.

This means the expectation of when you can see results and the reality of how soon your efforts will bring you the desired outcome are even more out of line than a couple of years ago when it was me standing in your shoes.

So, as you've reached this point in the book, I think it is safe to assume, you are desperate in your situation and are committed to taking the steps necessary to bring about the change you desire. You've also attached a certain credibility to everything I've shared from my experience with DBT and are optimistic that it will instigate change in your life. Therefore, I am asking you to be patient, kind to yourself, persistent in your efforts, and know that change is a choice you have to make every day of your life. Still, I would wake up every morning knowing and telling myself that living the life I deserve is a choice I have to make several times during my day.

DBT takes time and so does change. How much time it will take depends entirely on you. Every person is unique in personality, circumstances, the severity of their anger, and their expectations of the future. For some, DBT brings the results they are seeking within six months. Others sometimes work relentlessly for a year before they can notice significant differences. What makes it even harder is that at times these differences can be so subtle that it is easy to miss them. Therefore, keep track of your emotions and incidents in your journal as much as possible. Here, you'll be able to measure the change in your behavior far more effectively. Keep in mind that there are certain types of behavior and problematic symptoms that may stay with you even long after you've already invested a year into resolving them. The difference is thought that even if these symptoms remain around for longer than you want, you've disempowered them from having any control over your life as you are now fully equipped with all the skills you need to manage your emotions, especially anger, effectively.

Never judge yourself in where you are standing in the current moment for where you are heading is far more important. As long as you are facing in the right direction, you can be at peace that progress is happening at just the right pace for you.

You have the tools to empower yourself, and when you've reached this point of the book, I know that you've created a strong and sturdy foundation for weathering the storms life will send across your way with ease and success. Now, go forth, and gently introduce the world to the newer & greater version of you.

GLOSSARY

These definitions can also be found in my other book: DBT Skills and Mindfulness for Teen Anxiety: A Neurodivergent Friendly Guide for Emotional Regulation to Understand, Manage, and Prevent Toxic Emotions; Overcome Fear, Panic, and Worry

ACCEPTS:

ACCEPTS is a DBT skill that stands for activities, contributing, comparisons, emotions, pushing away, thoughts, and sensations. It is a skill used to distract your mind from obsessing over the cause of your anger.

AMYGDALA:

The amygdala is the area in the brain where we process memories, and it plays especially an important role in how we remember memories. It has the size and shape of two walnuts and is situated deeply in the brain's center.

BORDERLINE PERSONALITY DISORDER (BPD):

BDP is a mental disorder characterized by difficulty with emotion regulation, interpersonal functioning, and the stability of behavior. People with BPD may experience intense emotions, fear of abandonment, impulsive behaviors, and unstable relationships. DBT is an evidence-based form of treatment for BPD.

DEAR MAN:

DEAR MAN is a dialectical behavior therapy skill that stands for describe, express, assert, reinforce, mindful, appear, express, assert, reinforce, mindful, appear confident, and negotiate. It is used to help people learn how to be assertive in their communication with others.

DIALECTICAL BEHAVIOR THERAPY (DBT):

DBT is a type of talk therapy for people who experience emotions like anger intensely. The type of therapy relies on learning various skills to treat a range of mental health concerns like BPD, but it can also improve mental health in a range of other ways.

DISTRESS TOLERANCE:

The term refers to the ability to tolerate distressful emotions and experiences without making them worse. This includes learning how to control your reactions when faced with a difficult situation and developing the ability to ride out the storm until it passes.

FAST:

FAST is an interpersonal effectiveness skill acronym for fair; apology; sticking to values and facts; and truth. It can be used to help you stay focused on the important issues in a conversation and speak your truth respectfully.

GIVE:

GIVE is an interpersonal effectiveness skill acronym for gentle, interested, validating, and easy manner. It can help you communicate effectively in difficult situations.

GROUNDING:

Grounding refers to a set of skills to help you stay in the moment while feeling overwhelmed by feelings. By remaining in the present at the moment, it becomes easier to deal with distress.

INTERPERSONAL EFFECTIVENESS:

Interpersonal effectiveness refers to the ability to get what you want while maintaining, or even improving, relationships. It is a set of skills designed to help you communicate effectively and navigate social situations with ease.

MINDFULNESS:

Mindfulness is the practice of focusing on the present moment without judgment or analysis. It involves cultivating an awareness of your thoughts, feelings, and environment in order to gain insight into your feelings and sensations.

OPPOSITE ACTION:

This is an emotion regulation skill used to help you shift your emotional state in a way that is helpful and adaptive. It involves taking action that is the opposite of what your current emotion might suggest, such as forcing yourself to act cheerful when sad.

RADICAL ACCEPTANCE:

Radical acceptance is a practice of embracing and accepting the present moment without judgment or resistance. It allows you to acknowledge your feelings and experiences without getting caught up in the need to change them. In DBT, radical acceptance is one of the four core skills and can increase self-compassion.

RAIN:

RAIN is a DBT skill that stands for recognize, allow, investigate, and nonidentification. It is used to help people to face strong emotions by turning toward what they experience in a nonjudgmental way.

STOP:

STOP is an emotion regulation skill acronym that stands for stop, take a step back, observe the situation objectively, and proceed mindfully. It can help you stay mindful in difficult moments and make decisions based on what is best for you.

THINK:

THINK is an interpersonal effectiveness skill acronym that stands for think, have empathy, interpretations, notice, and kindness. It can help you communicate effectively in difficult situations.

TIPP:

TIPP is a distress tolerance skill acronym that stands for temperature, intense, exercise, paced breathing, and progressive muscle relaxation. It can help you cope with difficult emotions in a healthy way.

VALIDATION:

Validation is the process of recognizing and understanding another person's feelings and experiences without judgment or criticism. It can build relationships and foster greater empathy, understanding, and compassion between people. In DBT, validation is a core skill that can help you better understand yourself and others.

WISE MIND:

This is a concept that combines the logical and emotional aspects of the self. It encourages you to use both your rational and intuitive sides to make decisions, rather than relying on one or the other. In DBT, the wise mind serves as a guiding principle for making mindful, balanced decisions.

GET THIS EXCLUSIVE

5-minute Audio Guided Meditation

To help safely **MANAGE YOUR TEEN'S** sudden emotional meltdown.

and more mindfulness resources...

JOURNALS & SELF-CARE PLANERS

COLORING BOOKS

SCAN QR CODE TO GET YOUR COPY

MESSAGE FROM THE AUTHOR

I truly hope you found this book enjoyable and gained valuable insights from its contents.

If you could spare a moment to share your honest feedback or leave a star-rating on Amazon, I would greatly appreciate it.

(Rating only takes a few clicks).

Your review can guide other young adults to explore this book and potentially aid them on their personal journeys. Plus, it might just bring some good karma your way.

SCAN QR CODE TO GET YOUR COPY

REFERENCES

Ambrose. (2022, June 1). No one heals himself by wounding another [Quote]. Wisdom Quotes. https://wisdomquotes.com/anger-quotes/

American Psychology Association. (n.d.) Anger. https://www.apa.org/topics/anger#:~:text=Anger%20is%20an%20emotion%20characterized

American Psychology Association. (2011). Strategies for controlling your anger: Keeping anger in check. https://www.apa.org/topics/anger/strategies-controlling

Andrews, M. (n.d.). 10 types of anger: What's your anger style? Life Supports. https://lifesupportscounselling.com.au/resources/blogs/10-types-of-anger-what-s-your-anger-style/

Anwar, B. (2022, April 27). 4 DBT therapy techniques. Talkspace. https://www.talkspace.com/blog/dbt-therapy-techniques/

Attai, K. (2020, December 1). DBT: The emotional mind, the rational mind, and the wise mind. Living Well Counseling Services. https://livingwellcounselling.ca/dbt-emotional-mind-rational-mind-wise-mind/

Babauta, L. (n.d.). Learn to respond, not react. Zen Habits. https://zenhabits.net/respond/

Bajori, A. (2019, April 20). 8 types of anger: What they mean and what to do about them. Verv. https://verv.com/8-types-of-anger/

Balancing emotional urges. (n.d.). Dialectical Behavior Therapy. https://dialecticalbehaviortherapy.com/emotion-regulation/balancing-emotional-urges/

ABelcher, M. (2016, January 13). DBT skills: Moving through shame. Sunrise Residential Treatment Center. https://sunrisertc.com/dbt-skills-moving-through-shame/

BetterHelp Editorial Team. (2022, December 8). An overview of anger as an emotion. BetterHelp. https://www.betterhelp.com/advice/anger/what-is-anger-definition-psychology-behind-this-emotion/

Brach, T. (2019, February 7). Feeling overwhelmed? Remember RAIN. Mindful. https://www.mindful.org/tara-brach-rain-mindfulness-practice/

Bray, S. (2012, September 24). Managing your emotions through dialectical behavior therapy. GoodTherapy. https://www.goodtherapy.org/blog/managing-emotions-through-dialectical-behavior-therapy-0924124

Buddha. (n.d.-a). Holding on to anger is like grasping a hot coal with the intent of throwing it on someone else; you are the one who gets burned [Quote]. OutofStress. https://www.outofstress.com/calming-quotes-for-anger/

Buddha. (n.d.-b). Words have the power to both destroy and heal [Quote]. Tumblr. https://inspiredbywisdom.tumblr.com/post/181916778092/words-have-the-power-to-both-destroy-and-heal

Butler, L. (n.d.). 4 steps from DBT that can boost your self esteem. Bay Area Mental Health. https://support.bayareamentalhealth.com/kb/en/article/4-steps-from-dbt-that-can-boost-your-self-esteem

Camacho, N. A. (2021, December 23). Reacting and responding are different—And experts say one is much better for relationship health. Well+Good. https://www.wellandgood.com/reacting-versus-responding/

Cherry, K. (2022, September 2). Benefits of mindfulness. Verywell Mind. https://www.verywellmind.com/the-benefits-of-mindfulness-5205137

Cheung, L. (n.d.). Mindfully recognizing being overwhelmed already reduces the feeling of being overwhelmed [Pin]. Pinterest. https://za.pinterest.com/pin/327355466639072069/

Clear Concept. (2020, November 16). What does it mean to respond instead of react? Clear Concept Inc. https://clearconceptinc.ca/what-does-it-mean-to-respond-instead-of-react/

Cleveland Clinic. (n.d.). Dialectical behavior therapy (DBT). https://my.clevelandclinic.org/health/treatments/22838-dialectical-behavior-therapy-dbt

The costs and pay-offs of anger. (n.d.). Mainstream Corporate Training. https://mainstreamcorporatetraining.com/the-costs-and-pay-offs-of-anger/

The cycle of anger. (n.d.). The Wellness Corner. https://www.thewellnesscorner.com/blog/the-cycle-of-anger

Dialectical behaviour therapy (DBT). (n.d.). Centre for Addiction and Mental Health. https://www.camh.ca/en/health-info/mental-illness-and-addiction-index/dialectical-behaviour-therapy

Distract with wise mind ACCEPTS. (n.d.). DBT Self-Help. https://dbtselfhelp.com/dbt-skills-list/distress-tolerance/accepts/

Dorter, G. (n.d.). DBT Skills: Wise mind, emotional mind and reasonable mind. Greg Dorter Counselling and Therapy. https://www.guelphtherapist.ca/blog/dbt-skills-wise-mind-emotional-mind-and-reasonable-mind/

Do you recognize the 10 types of anger? (n.d.). Montreal CBT Psychologist.
https://www.montrealcbtpsychologist.com/blog/122622-do-you-recognize-the-10-types-of-anger_8

Eddins, R. (2020, April 1). Grounding techniques & Self soothing for emotional regulation. Eddins Counseling Group.
https://eddinscounseling.com/grounding-techniques-self-soothing-emotional-regulation/

8 ways to deal with anger. (n.d.). ReachOut.
https://au.reachout.com/articles/8-ways-to-deal-with-anger

Elliott, C. H., Smith, L. L., & Gentry, W. D. (2016, March 26). The costs and benefits of your anger. Dummies.
https://www.dummies.com/article/body-mind-spirit/emotional-health-psychology/emotional-health/anger-management/the-costs-and-benefits-of-your-anger-141936/

Greene, P. (2020, August 3). The DBT STOP skill: How to not make a bad situation worse. Manhattan Center for Cognitive Behavioral Therapy.
https://www.manhattancbt.com/archives/1723/dbt-stop-skill/

Holland, K. (2019, January 29). How to control anger: 25 tips to help you stay calm. Healthline.
https://www.healthline.com/health/mental-health/how-to-control-anger

Holmes, O. W. (n.d.). The great thing in this world is not so much where you stand as what direction you are moving [Quote]. Landmark Recovery.
https://landmarkrecovery.com/addiction-recovery-quotes/

Imagine Boise. (2022, March 11). How can DBT help my teen? Imagine Boise.
https://www.boiseimagine.com/mental-health-blog/how-can-dbt-help-my-teen/

Kriegler, S. (2020, December 1). Dialectical behaviour therapy: Reasonable mind, emotion mind & wise mind. Dr Susan Kriegler.
https://www.susankriegler.com/post/cbt-reasonable-mind-emotion-mind-wise-mind

Lifford, T. (n.d.). When you know yourself you are empowered. When you accept yourself you are invincible [Quote]. Quotesgram.
https://quotesgram.com/you-know-who-you-are-quotes/

Linehan, M. (n.d.). STOP skill. DBT Tools.
https://dbt.tools/emotional_regulation/stop.php

Mind. (2018, July). How to manage angry outbursts.
https://www.mind.org.uk/information-support/types-of-mental-health-problems/anger/managing-outbursts/

Mind. (2020, December). Dialectical behaviour therapy.
https://www.mind.org.uk/information-support/drugs-and-treatments/talking-therap
y-and-counselling/dialectical-behaviour-therapy-dbt/

mindfulness. (n.d.). Opposite to emotion Action: A DBT skill to reduce problem
behaviors. Mindfulness Therapy Associates.
https://mindfulnesstherapy.org/opposite-to-emotion-action/

Mitts, C. (2018, February 5). Understanding anger triggers. Ipseity Counseling
Clinic.
https://ipseitycounselingclinic.com/2018/02/05/understanding-anger-triggers/

Moore, M. (2022, July 7). 4 DBT skills for everyday challenges. Psych Central.
https://psychcentral.com/health/dbt-skills-therapy-techniques

Nelson, S. (2021, June 18). 8 ways to help maintain emotional balance. Rest Less.
https://restless.co.uk/health/healthy-mind/8-ways-to-help-maintain-emotional-balance/

Newport Academy. (2022, June 24). What is DBT for teens and how does it
work?
https://www.newportacademy.com/resources/mental-health/what-is-dbt/#:~:text=
DBT%20teaches%20teens%20how%20choosing

O'Brien, M. (n.d.). R.A.I.N: A four-step process for using mindfulness in difficult
times. Melli O'Brien.
https://melliobrien.com/r-n-four-step-process-using-mindfulness-difficult-times/

Ohwovoriole, T. (2021, May 28). What is anger? Verywell Mind.
https://www.verywellmind.com/what-is-anger-5120208

Out of Home Care Toolbox. (n.d.). Understand and recognise triggers.
https://www.oohctoolbox.org.au/understand-and-recognise-triggers

Peterson, T. J. (2022, November 25). Meditation for anger: How it works & tips
for getting started. Choosing Therapy.
https://www.choosingtherapy.com/meditation-for-anger/

Physiology of anger. (n.d.). MentalHelp.net.
https://www.mentalhelp.net/anger/physiology/

Pickford, M. (n.d.). The past cannot be changed. The future is yet in your power
[Quote]. Goodreads.
https://www.goodreads.com/quotes/44866-the-past-cannot-be-changed-the-future
-is-yet-in

Pieper, J. (2022, November 24). DBT for teens: How it works, examples &
effectiveness. Choosing Therapy. https://www.choosingtherapy.com/dbt-for-teens/

Promises Behavioral Health. (2022, August 22). Physical signs of anger.
https://www.promises.com/addiction-blog/physical-signs-of-anger/

Radical acceptance & turning the mind. (n.d.). DBT Self-Help.
https://dbtselfhelp.com/dbt-skills-list/distress-tolerance/radical-acceptance/

Raypole, C. (2020, April 28). How to become the boss of your emotions.
Healthline. https://www.healthline.com/health/how-to-control-your-emotions

Recognizing anger signs. (n.d.). MentalHelp.net.
https://www.mentalhelp.net/anger/recognizing-signs/

Rista, M. (2021, February 20). Mindfulness of current emotions. The Behavioral
Therapy Collective.
https://thebehavioraltherapycollective.com/blog/2021/2/20/mindfulness-of-current-
emotions

Schenck, L. K. (n.d.). What is "wise mind?" Mindfulness Muse.
https://www.mindfulnessmuse.com/dialectical-behavior-therapy/what-is-wise-mind

Shenoy, S. (2018, June 1). How to find balance when you're emotionally triggered.
The Dream Catcher.
https://thedreamcatch.com/find-balance-when-youre-emotionally-triggered/

A simple formula for responding not reacting. (n.d.). The Growth Equation.
https://thegrowtheq.com/a-simple-formula-for-responding-not-reacting/#:~:text=R
eacting%20is%20quick

Skedel, R. (2022, November 28). 12 types of anger. Choosing Therapy.
https://www.choosingtherapy.com/types-of-anger/

Skyland Trail. (2019, October 28). Accepting reality using DBT skills.
https://www.skylandtrail.org/accepting-reality-using-dbt-skills/

Sukel, K. (2018, March 13). Beyond emotion: Understanding the amygdala's role in
memory. Dana Foundation.
https://dana.org/article/beyond-emotion-understanding-the-amygdalas-role-in-mem
ory/#:~:text=The%20amygdalae%2C%20a%20pair%20of

Sullivan, K. (2018, November 28). Mindfulness of current emotion. Accessible
DBT. https://accessibledbt.com/mindfulness-of-current-emotion/

sunriserTC. (2017a, August 18). DBT interpersonal effectiveness skills: The guide
to healthy relationships. Sunrise Residential Treatment Center.
https://sunrisertc.com/interpersonal-effectiveness/

sunriserTC. (2017b, September 13). DBT Distress tolerance skills: Your 6-skill
guide to navigate emotional crises. Sunrise Residential Treatment Center.
https://sunrisertc.com/distress-tolerance-skills/

Tayloe, D. (2022, April 26). 7 ways to unlearn bad habits that harm mental health.
Power of Positivity.
https://www.powerofpositivity.com/unlearn-bad-habits-that-harm-mental-health/

Tolle, E. (n.d.). Where there is anger, there is always pain underneath [Quote]. Quotefancy. https://quotefancy.com/anger-quotes

Vassar, G. (2011, March 1). Do you know your anger triggers? Lakeside. https://lakesidelink.com/blog/do-you-know-your-anger-triggers/

What is anger? (n.d.). Mentalhelp.net. https://www.mentalhelp.net/anger/what-is-it/
What is radical acceptance in DBT? (2021, September 29). Cyti Clinics. https://cyticlinics.com/what-is-radical-acceptance-in-dbt/

Winona State University. (2016, November 21). Grounding. https://www.winona.edu/resilience/Media/Grounding-Worksheet.pdf

IMAGE REFERENCES

Andrea Cassani. (2022, May 20). [Red image of woman grimacing] [Image]. Unsplash. https://unsplash.com/photos/0eekd4benvc

Andres Siimon. (2020, September 18). Man with magnifying glass [Image]. Unsplash. https://unsplash.com/photos/Oe3JidQ9UvU

Ása Steinarsdóttir. (2021, March 31). Erupting volcano in Iceland [Image]. Unsplash. https://unsplash.com/photos/_xmAPHUXXiU

Barry Weatherall. (2019, August 14). Waiting for the big show... [Image]. Unsplash. https://unsplash.com/photos/Hm_iFim94bw

Benjamin Wedemeyer. (2021, April 19). A young artist paints his dreams in his own world [Image]. Unsplash. https://unsplash.com/photos/hicQxC0SyVc

Ethan Rheams. (2018, August 28). [Trees beside body of water] [Image]. Unsplash. https://unsplash.com/photos/sSOYcNt3R54

Giulia Bertelli. (2016, May 20). Crossed hands [Image]. Unsplash. https://unsplash.com/photos/dvXGnwnYweM

Joshua Hoehne. (2019, November 1). [Selective photography of stop signage] [Image]. Unsplash. https://unsplash.com/photos/WPrTKRw8KRQ

Kelly Sikkema. (2020, January 16). Man handing a woman a heart shape [Image]. Unsplash. https://unsplash.com/photos/XX2WTbLr3r8

Lina Trochez. (2017, September 14). Brindar siempre lo mejor de ti [Image]. Unsplash. https://unsplash.com/photos/ktPKyUs3Qjs

Liz Weddon. (2018, March 16). [Gray empty locker room] [Image]. Unsplash. https://unsplash.com/photos/XrYS3pjzHhU

Markus Winkler. (2020, June 7). [Black flatscreen TV turned onto yellow emoji] [Image]. Unsplash. https://unsplash.com/photos/wpOa2i3MUrY

Michal Matlon. (2021, February 21). [White sheep on white surface] [Image]. Unsplash. https://unsplash.com/photos/4ApmfdVo32Q

Miguel Bandeira. (2020, November 1). [Persons hand on body of water] [Image]. Unsplash. https://unsplash.com/photos/6vHGBZ2A5Rc

Mike Enerio. (2016, April 28). [Ariel view of grass] [Image]. Unsplash. https://unsplash.com/photos/H58bnmnedTc

Natasha Connel. (2019, August 24). [Brain figurine] [Image]. Unsplash. https://unsplash.com/photos/byp5TTxUbL0

Sergei Wing. (2020, June 9). Lake in a volcano crater at the Azores islands [Image]. Unsplash. https://unsplash.com/photos/ZqZfY4IFqRI

Sydney Rae. (2017, October 10). [Brown dried leaves on sand]. [Image]. Unsplash. https://unsplash.com/photos/geM5IzDj4Iw

Tingey Injury Law Firm. (2020, May 15). Lady Justice [Image]. Unsplash. https://unsplash.com/photos/L4YGuSg0fxs

Volkan Olmez. (2014, April 13). Female head from behind [Image]. Unsplash. https://unsplash.com/photos/wESKMSgZJDo

Made in United States
Orlando, FL
07 May 2025